# Pregnancy
# and
# Abortion
# Practical Guide

'Everyone should have this guide. We young people don't know this stuff.'

—A bar attendant in their 20s at the launch of the first edition

# Reviews from the First Edition

(*Pregnancy and Abortion: Your Choice*, 2017)

'I read it straight through, cover to cover, twice.'

High-school girl, aged 18, January 2018

'What a fresh approach to such a divisive issue. This book is non-judgemental, clearly laid-out, and easy to read... Gives hope whether pre- or post-abortion. I thoroughly recommend it.'

Website review, 27-year-old woman, November 2017

'Thanks for such a practical book to aid people in a very challenging decision! It takes the reader through the decision-making process and the options available. Your book was required reading on our course and the participants gave this feedback:

- The book is easy to read and dip in and out of.
- The book is completely open and non-judgemental.
- The information is handled in a factual but gentle way.
- The chapter on men and abortion is eye opening.
- The breast cancer chapter is interesting.'

Rebecca Johnson, Pregnancy Counselling tutor, Image, Manchester, UK, 18 June 2018

'Well written and readable, for physicians, parents, teens and older on the topic of abortion and pregnancy. The well-organised chapters consist of excellent questions with thoughtful and easily understood answers. Great read!'

Prof. Byron C. Calhoun, MD, FACOG, FACS, FASAM, MBA, 17 October 2018

'Thoroughly enjoyed your book... a concise and easy-to-understand guide for difficult choices.'

Martyn McCaffrey, MD, Capt. USN (Ret), Professor of Pediatrics in the Division of Neonatal-Perinatal Medicine at the University of North Carolina School of Medicine, 10 April 2019

# Pregnancy
## and
# Abortion

Practical Guide to Making Decisions

Dr Mark Houghton
with
Dr Esther Lüthy and Christine Fidler

Guest Author, Prof. John Wyatt,
Emeritus Professor of Neonatal Paediatrics,
University College London

Grace & Down
PUBLISHING

First published in 2017 as *Pregnancy and Abortion: Your Choice*
by Dr M. Houghton, Dr Esther Lüthy and Prof. John Wyatt

Grace and Down Publishing, an imprint of Malcolm Down Publishing Ltd
www.malcolmdown.co.uk

**IMPORTANT MEDICAL NOTICE**
Every care has been taken to ensure accurate information in this guide, but this guide is not a substitute for personal medical advice to any reader. Any reader wishing for medical advice should consult his or her own medical practitioner in matters relating to their health and specifically with respect to any symptoms that may require diagnosis or medical attention.

Before any form of medical treatment, you should always consult your personal medical practitioner. In particular, (without limit) you should note that advances in medical science occur rapidly and some information about procedures, drugs and treatment in this book may soon be out of date.

We take care to select tested websites but we cannot take any responsibility for website content nor that of links you may go to.

**British Library Cataloguing in Publication Data**
A catalogue record for this book is available from the British Library.

ISBN 978-1-912863-19-8

Cover design by Esther Kotecha
Art direction by Sarah Grace

Printed in Great Britain by Bell and Bain Ltd, Glasgow

# Dedication

To pregnant women and their nearest

Sales profits go to resource pregnant women

> Before making decisions
> check out your hopes, dreams, risks and options.
> You have more options than you think.

We welcome comments and factual corrections.
If verified we will publish them at www.choicescommunity.co.uk –
after all, no one has all the answers, nor, despite every care over this
guide, can we get it all right.

Online updates by chapter are at www.choicescommunity.co.uk

 Facebook at www.Facebook.com/thechoicescommunity/

# Contents

# A Guide for You

Whether you are a pregnant woman, her partner, her parent, her friend or a professional – a pregnancy poses several decisions to be made. Every decision we make in life is a balance between two sides.

## Burdens v. Benefits

This involves weighing up what will be lost versus what could be gained. In pregnancy there are lots of unknowns to be checked out and lots of decisions affecting your future.

This process takes some thought, time and effort – but doing this now will help you make informed decisions for your future.

There are so many 'megaphone messages' we're surrounded with from opposite sides, either for or against abortion. When you're in the middle of deciding, it can feel uncomfortable between these extreme options.

Instead, we want to help you find answers during this time, so this guide offers you the following:

**Are you a pregnant woman?** This guide will help you think clearly, review your life from all angles and collect information for informed decisions on the road to your best option.

**Considering all options?** Your information is here in one place – readable, reliable and respectful towards you.

**Partner of a pregnant woman?** Are you a relative or friend? This equips you to support, listen and guide.

**Feeling under pressure to abort?** Sadly, coercion and 'non-choice' are common. This handbook can empower you to stand firm for your own decision.

**Have you already made up your mind?** Do you need to check some facts and risks? Go to the Contents.

**After abortion?** Do you feel fear, guilt or regret? Here is help and no condemnation. Perhaps you're struggling to find peace – after-abortion counselling is effective and available in Appendix 2 'Finding Help.'

**Are you a pastor or professional?** Sit with your client and work together using the counselling road map (in Part 1) – or they work alone and come back to chat more.

**Policymakers needing soundbites?** You have rapid access to online, cited, peer-reviewed information to cut and paste in minutes.

# A Guide Here to Help

**Miriam's visit to her doctor could be your story...**

*'I can't believe I'm pregnant! I'm thinking about abortion.'* Miriam's mind was made up, she said – yet I could see 'dilemma' written all over her face.

- How could I help her come to an informed choice in a short time?

- How could she gather and arrange the facts and feelings for informed choice?

- What resources could I find *now* to support her?

From stories like Miriam's came this guide – created by a team of doctors, professional female counsellors, and nurses as well as the stories of women and men, and those who have had abortions.

Neither birth, parenting, adoption nor ending a pregnancy are easy options – but this guide is our pledge, 'Here to help.'

# Overview at a Glance

**Part 1: The Journey to a Decision** is a step - by - step guide to making choices. In five short steps (chapters 2 – 6), Christine Fidler, an experienced pregnancy counsellor, helps you organise your hopes and fears, problems and resources.

Take your time over this. It's not easy to make the right decision for you when your head and your heart may be saying different things.

By the end you will have made exciting discoveries, including your strengths, which will help equip you to make a decision.

**Part 2: Exploring Your Options and Essential Facts** completes the journey to making *informed* decisions. There are numerous scenarios and options in an unintended pregnancy. In this section you will find information to explore which option will be best for you. Information helps solve the underlying problem.

This includes weighing the potential physical and emotional consequences ahead, using medical evidence.

**Part 3: Informing Choice by Digging Deeper** provides more facts especially for professionals – much of it not taught in academic circles – on the unintended after-effects for women, men and their future children.

**Appendix 1 'An ABC of Spiritual Beliefs'** covers the main faiths, including atheism, and how they can help make decisions, bring hope and deal with issues like guilt and death.

**Appendix 2 'Finding Help'** lists resources before or after abortion or other pregnancy loss. Much of this help is free, but abortion providers are usually commercial – the latter are easily found by local adverts.

**'Notes'** are empty pages for you to capture your thoughts and feelings.

# Introduction

Pregnancy can bring shock and confusion at any age or stage of life.

Whether you are a frightened 15-year-old, a five-times mother or had five abortions, each pregnancy brings unique challenges and decisions. Our guide helps you explore a path to your life ahead for your benefit.

Our combined expertise brings you the benefits of decades of face-to-face clinical counselling. We've seen the tried and tested roadmap (in chapters 2–6) helping women and their partners journey to the best decision for them. We have consulted with medical specialists at the top of their profession on both sides of the Atlantic.

The terms pregnancy, or fetus, or embryo, or baby, or unborn, or child get used in various situations for the pregnancy. As in real life, we have tried to use the 'best fit' for the situation. If you are not comfortable with a term in this guide we can only apologise.

We wish you the very best – better-informed with better understanding of your options and what a choice will bring in the years ahead.

# Part 1
# The Journey to a Decision

## Quick guide to Part 1

This is a step-by-step journey to gather your thoughts in order; then you will finish in a better place to make your own decisions.

If you have confirmed pregnancy jump to chapter 2. If you are not sure read chapter 1 here.

# Chapter 1
# Am I Pregnant?

## This chapter covers:

## 1.  Pregnancy tests

First things first – check if you are actually pregnant. Usually a missed period is the first sign of pregnancy, but a missed period can be caused by feeling upset or an illness.

Remember to make a note of the date of your *last menstrual period* (LMP) as this could be useful later.

Light bleeding or spotting of blood can seem like a period, when in fact it is the first missed period of a pregnancy.

Pregnancy test kits are cheap and sold from pharmacies and supermarkets. Read the instructions in the packet. They show a pregnancy by detecting the hormone HCG in a woman's urine after she falls pregnant.

For reliability, wait until the day of your missed period before testing.

---

**Getting a pregnancy test**

Pregnancy test kits cost a few dollars online.

UK pharmacies sell kits from about £1.50. NHS family doctors will test for free.

---

**Positive pregnancy test**

## 2. How reliable are pregnancy tests?

A *positive* test (saying you are pregnant) is almost certainly correct.

A *negative* test (you are not pregnant) is not so reliable. If your test is negative then it is best to test again in two or three days. If you keep getting negative results but you think you could be pregnant, see your doctor.

If you get a positive test on the first day of your missed period, it's probably about two weeks since you conceived.

Pregnancy tests from a blood sample can be positive a few days before the urine pregnancy test and can be obtained from your family doctor. More information can be found at the NHS website.[1]

## 3. Pregnancy – what is happening inside you?

Each month a woman releases an egg from her ovary, and this is called *mid-cycle ovulation*.

If a couple has sex and the man's sperm bonds with the woman's egg deep inside her, she 'falls pregnant'. That's about eight days before her next period. A human embryo starts, and this is called fertilisation or conception. This embryo attaches to the womb – at 'implantation' – six to 12 days after mid-cycle ovulation (more on this in chapter 7 'Week-by-week of Pregnancy').

A positive blood test for pregnancy can occur as early as three or four days after implantation bleeding, and four or five days before a missed period. This small implantation bleeding – or 'show' – can be mistaken for a period. The NHS website has a chart for these stages of the embryo.[2]

## 4. Signs of being pregnant

Other clues that can suggest pregnancy are:

- Stomach cramps
- Urinating more often
- A strange metallic taste in the mouth
- Feeling very tired
- Feeling sick, often in the mornings but also at other times of day
- Breasts getting larger and more sensitive.

## 5. Caution – ectopic pregnancy

If you have tummy (abdominal) pain in early pregnancy, call a doctor urgently, as this may signal an ectopic pregnancy where the embryo has implanted outside your uterus in the wrong place. An untreated ectopic pregnancy can threaten your life.

Other symptoms of ectopic pregnancy can be:

- Pain in one shoulder tip
- Pain when passing urine for a 'pee' or doing a 'poo'
- Diarrhoea
- Vaginal bleeding or discharge looking a bit like 'prune juice' from canned prunes.

## Bursting of an ectopic

A burst (or ruptured) ectopic is *an emergency* and signs are:

- Sudden sharp pain in your tummy
- Collapsing or feeling dizzy, faint and looking very pale
- Feeling sick or vomiting.

**Act now: call for an emergency ambulance** or go to your nearest hospital Emergency Room (A&E).

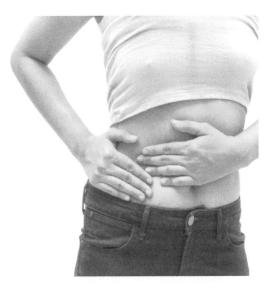

**Is the pain an ectopic pregnancy?**

When pregnant, you may not feel any different from usual, but you can still be pregnant.

## 6. What about pregnancy without full intercourse?

Perhaps you are thinking you can't be pregnant because you didn't have full intercourse, or your partner withdrew from you before his climax.

However, you can still become pregnant this way, since some sperm may escape and swim up the vagina to your womb, even from your outer private parts.

## 7. Can I get pregnant while on contraception?

Yes, while contraception is effective when properly used, in real life with excitements and forgetfulness, pregnancy can happen such as when:

- The condom breaks or falls off during sex. In a year of use about 1 in 5 women will conceive.
- The contraceptive Pill may fail while on medication such as antibiotics, having tummy upsets, vomiting and diarrhoea. In real life about 1 woman in 10 will fall pregnant while using the Pill for a year.
- Using the patch or injection of Depo-Provera about 6 to 10 women out of 100 will conceive in a year of use.
- The Morning After Pill (MAP) fails in up to a third of uses for various reasons.[3]
- Implanted long-acting reversible contraceptives (LARCs) and coils allow pregnancy for up to 1 woman in 100 during a year's use or from the replacement date being forgotten or the device falls out.[4]

## 8. Morning After Pill (MAP)

The MAP, also called Post Coital Contraception (PCC) and Emergency Contraception (EC), may work if used in the first five days after having sex. 'Although EC can prevent unintended pregnancy for an individual woman, it has failed to make an impact on abortion rates at a population level.'[5]

Usually the MAP stops the human embryo settling into the wall of the womb (implantation). This stops the feeding of the embryo, which is expelled through the vagina.

The MAP is not to be confused with Medical Abortion (also called the Abortion Pill) covered in chapter 10, 'Abortion Explored'.

# Chapter 2
# I'm Pregnant – What Next?

Step one to a decision is in this chapter. It is for those with a confirmed pregnancy and covers:

1. My thoughts, feelings and talking it over
2. Mood, body and mind swings
3. Tunnel vision
4. Things to do next
5. Questions you may be asking

## 1.  My thoughts, feelings and talking it over

You may have questions like 'Why now? Why me? How come, when we used protection?' Feelings of disbelief are often the first response.

Perhaps you are wondering who you want to tell, and how they will respond, or there may be a question of whose baby this is.

On the other hand, you may just feel numb and unable to think – like Isabella, who told me,

> 'I couldn't do anything for two weeks but sit in my room and just keep going to school.'

You may be feeling relieved that you can get pregnant and you are happy that you are – or even feel both delight and fear!

Give yourself time to settle while you process what has happened, and give it some thought, guided by the simple steps in chapters 3 to 6.

Think over someone you can talk to – a friend or family member. The ideal person is one who can take a surprise calmly, and you can count on them not to be critical or pushy. Someone who listens well and won't rush you into action you may regret is of great value.

Like Isabella, listen to what your heart is saying and be ready to stand up to those who will disagree with your decision...

You may feel more confident talking with someone distant – perhaps on a phone helpline. More info on helplines is in Appendix 2 'Finding Help', at the back of this guide.

Taking folic acid vitamin 10mg a day is a safe and simple way for pregnant women to prevent most spina bifida problems in a fetus. While it is best started even before conceiving, you should start taking this as soon as possible for your situation.

## 2. Mood, body and mind swings

As your body rapidly adapts, your moods may go high and low from one minute to the next. It's common to shoot up in elation and then to plummet to tearfulness and confusion. Such emotions can add to the problem of thinking clearly. Uncertainty can rise and cause you to swing from one decision to the next quicker than you can finish a cup of coffee.

## 3. Tunnel vision

The shock of an unintended pregnancy can be overwhelming, like a dark tunnel – where has the light gone? Perhaps there is a faint light at the end of the tunnel to do with making up your mind – but the question is, how to do that?

This 'tunnel vision' can make you long to turn the clock back and go back to the simple happy state you were in. But the road is going only one way; your life has changed, and we must face up to what to do next – and *there is a next*, believe it or not.

Whatever decision you make, this will become part of your life experience. There is a life after pregnancy, so let's find it.

Don't be surprised if 'tunnel vision' feels like fear as the time to decide draws nearer. And it may feel like your usual inner resources in difficulty have vanished, but that's okay. Also, it may be hard to imagine life at the other end of the tunnel. Just carry on reading.

## 4. Things to do next

Having covered some basics, the next chapter 'Setting Out' is the first step to a decision. Over four short chapters you will find your inner strengths, your outer resources and apply them to your own situation for a solution.

Even if you are feeling fine, experience suggests it's wise to do these steps and check out the facts in Part 2 before making a final decision. Most people are not well informed of the after-effects of abortion and the practical options.

## 5. Questions you may be asking

- What are my options?
- What am I going to do?
- Do I know the real pros and cons of parenting or adoption or abortion?

The rest of this guide helps you find answers, so you will come to a decision better informed.

**In our experience, women and men who decide in this way are usually more at peace in their future lives.**

# Chapter 3
# Setting Out

**Now we have covered falling pregnant, this chapter covers:**

1. Using the pressure you feel
2. The Journey to Decision
3. Starting the journey

## 1. Using the pressure you feel

'A journey of a thousand miles begins with a single step.'
(Chinese proverb)

You may find making decisions difficult at the best of times, and a pregnancy decision can be overwhelming. But this pressure can bring out your best and propel you to a helpful look at your life.

Sharing your news with others may have brought strong reactions from your partner, friends or family – closely followed by so called 'good advice'.

Your partner may say, *'I'll support you whatever you decide,'* just when you'd like them to shoulder the weight of this big issue and give some direction.

## 2. The Journey to Decision

The picture below is an aid that has helped many to make sense of it all.

Put yourself at the start of that journey and have a look at the next parking place coming up. There is a journey to go through before you arrive at the roundabout and make the decision.

Don't worry too much about how long it takes; the different stages on the journey can sometimes be done in less than a day and sometimes need weeks. The time it takes *you* to complete this journey is what matters.

## Journey to Decision

## 3. Starting the journey

Find a quiet space with some pen and paper. As you can see in the picture there are five stages or places to pause at.

Look at the five stops (layovers) in the picture:

1. **'Explore situation'** helps you to look at your life now from all angles (more details in chapter 4 'Your Resources').
2. **'Look at options** helps you see that although any decision brings challenges – there are other options and solutions (chapter 5 'Your Options').
3. **'Gains and losses'** is a method of weighing up what each decision could cost or gain you (we are still in chapter 5 'Your Options').
4. **'Information'** is about equipping you with essential facts such as the side-effects of abortion before you commit to a decision (more details in Part 2).
5. **'What next?'** (chapter 6 'Nearing Decision Time') is about when to decide, feelings and regrets – the information unique for you, so that you can make a better final decision.

**Journey alone or together?** It is important that after you have worked through the stages of the journey, the decision you come to is yours. If a partner is journeying with you, try to involve them. Others will have to know sooner or later and be involved.

The support of a trained pregnancy counsellor can help you apply the aids in this guide or you may turn to a trusted friend. You may want someone else to make notes while you talk.

Beware of thinking that all this can be done by staff at abortion clinics. Many are caring, but reports show that pressure of time and commercial interests reduce the quality of counselling and information for an informed decision.[1]

# Chapter 4
# Your Resources

Here we uncover your desires, resources and strengths – it's the first layover, called 'Explore situation', after starting the journey to decision.

1. Exploring your situation
2. Using the 4H Tool:
   a. What's happened?
   b. What's going on in your head?
   c. What's going on in your heart?
   d. What do you bring in your hands?
3. Reviewing your situation

## 1.  Exploring your situation

We will unpack the conflicting thoughts which make a decision about a pregnancy difficult. This will make things clearer to move forward.

---

**Claire's story**

Claire is 20 years old, in her second year at university and enjoying her studies.

She has been on the pill but forgot to take it a couple of times and has just found out she is pregnant. She has only known her boyfriend for six months and doesn't want to tell him.

Her mum was pregnant as a teenager and had encouraged her to go on the pill, so she doesn't want to tell her either.

She feels devastated that this has happened and annoyed at herself. She is thinking of having an abortion.

---

Now let's use the 4H Tool to help you see your personal situation; it's helped many women make sense of where they are now.

## 2. Using the 4H Tool

Think of your life from 4 aspects –

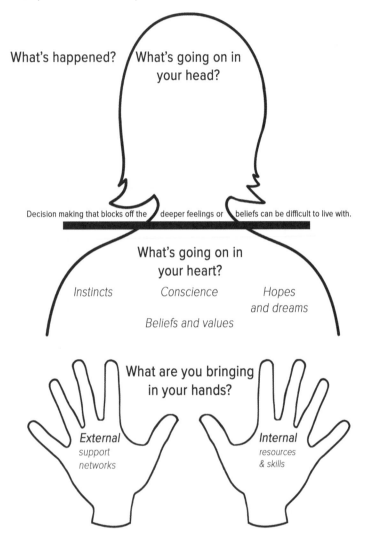

The tool contains four words that represent different parts of your situation, as in the diagram above.

a. Happened
b. Head

c. Heart

d. Hands

Happened and Hands, the first and the last, are more about what is going on in your *outside* circumstances; Head and Heart, the middle two, are exploring what is going on *inside* your mind and at a deeper level inside you.

At the end of the chapter you will find a completed diagram, using Claire's example, and a blank diagram for you to fill in yourself. Take a sheet with the blank 4H Tool on page 41 and begin now while you read the notes below.

### a. What's happened?

'What's happened?' may seem like an odd question. You obviously know what's happened and you may feel like you don't need to write it down. But it is surprisingly helpful to get your feelings out in the open. And if you are working through this with someone, it is helpful for them to know what's happened. So, write in the space around the head (as in the completed example below) all the circumstances that have impacted your pregnancy.

Be specific and put down the *facts* of your situation. For instance, you may be at school, in full-time education, have a good job, not be sure who the father is, have no money, have no plans to have a child now, or several of these may apply. List all the circumstances making you anxious.

### b. What's going on in your head?

Our minds are great at taking in the things going on around us, so the head in the diagram should show our situation.

What thoughts are constantly going through your mind about this pregnancy? Write inside the head space what you are thinking. Try to identify the thought patterns that keep repeating inside your head.

Note down *why* you're thinking these things at any one time. For instance, you may be telling yourself,

'No one must know,' or

'I'm going to lose my partner if I don't make a certain decision,' or

'I couldn't manage,' or

'I don't want a baby now,' or

'My parents will kill me!' or

'How could I be so stupid?'

You may also be feeling sure about what you want to do.

Once you have written down your thoughts, pause to consider a few things:

- If you are feeling pressure, where or who is that coming from? From your job, your parent(s) or from who?
- Is it genuine pressure now, or what you are anxious might happen? One woman told me, 'I fear he will throw me out if he finds out I am pregnant.' Another said, 'I am a Muslim; pregnancy outside of marriage is treated very seriously – what will happen?'
- What would need to change to release some of that pressure?
- Are you feeling that you have been given options? If there are no options, there is no real choice.
- Are you under coercion to get rid of the pregnancy?

Whether you feel it or not, there are options and choices, and they are yours to be had.

### c. What's going on in your heart?

The 'heart' means anything that is happening inside you. This may include your instincts, values and beliefs. Also, the heart holds your hopes and dreams ahead.

The heart holds those things that are deep-rooted within us and helps to define who we are and how we see ourselves. The heart is a deep well from which spring up desires, plans and purposes. It helps shape where we want to be in five- or ten-years' time.

Ask yourself, is there anything else going on for me at any other level regarding this pregnancy? For instance, try saying this phrase out loud and finish it in your own words, *'Deep down in my heart I know that...'*

Quite likely you finished with a personal value like, 'It's my right to choose,' or 'I don't want to bring a child into the world alone,' or 'I was always pro-life, but now it's me...' or 'I want to be a mother, but I can't see how.'

Spiritual values that serve us are very important. Hundreds of studies show the health gains of living by by the faith you believe and the damage from breaking your deep beliefs. (See more in Appendix 1 'ABC of Spiritual Beliefs'.)

It may be that when you first discovered you were pregnant you were excited. You may have started to connect with this pregnancy and are already thinking and imagining the future if you were to continue.

Perhaps you have always wanted a baby, but the timing is difficult. You may have had strong beliefs and values about the unborn and abortion before you became pregnant; now you feel the conflict as you consider breaking those beliefs.

Maybe none of these apply to you, but you may recognise that there are some uncomfortable thoughts or feelings as you consider an option. **Write it all in the Heart area** – anything that reflects deeply held values.

**The good thing** is that decision-making involving every aspect of our lives will generally lead us to decisions that we can live with. When the head and the heart agree, there is no internal conflict about the course of action.

But decision-making that blocks off deeper beliefs is more likely to lead to conflicts later. The support provided to those who have had an abortion confirms this.

So now ask yourself, does anything in your Heart area conflict with what is in your Head area? If so, think about the decision in terms of how you may feel if you go against your heart. How will that affect you as a person? How might that affect you in the future and the child you want?

**d.  What do you bring in your hands?**

This is about who or what resources that can support you in this situation, including your own personal strengths (and weaknesses). Rest assured, we find *everyone* – yes including you – has strengths.

Use one of the hands to write down what your *external* support networks are, such as a partner, family, or friends. Put here, too, any support you can get from organisations, such as social care, crisis pregnancy centres with baby clothes and a safe house, or counselling. Are any of these support networks relevant to your decision? If yes, in what way?

Use the other hand to write down what *internal* resources you are bringing to the situation – or feel you *don't have*. This could be a strength, such as being determined and independent, or maybe a weakness you are prone to like depression and struggles with mental health.

You may have a skill, such as being good with children – will you grow as a person once that skill has an outlet?

You can copy and fill in the blank 4H Tool (two pages on) for your own situation.

## 3. Reviewing your situation

By now, you may need a coffee to pause a while and review your situation and resources!

After filling in the blank 4H Tool, read over it and consider what you have found:

- Where are you at?
- What are you bringing to this situation?
- Look for any conflicting feelings that have come up. What will resolve those feelings?
- What information gaps need filling?

## What's happened?

- I'm 20.
- Enjoying University
- Boyfriend - for
  6 months.
- Pill but forgot it a couple of
  times.
- Two weeks overdue -
  positive pregnancy test
- Can't tell Mum, she was
  a pregnant teenager
  and wanted better for
  me.
- Was enjoying life - now
  feel devastated.

### What's going on in my head?

An abortion would mean I
don't have to tell my
boyfriend or my mum and I
can carry on with my studies.

I feel stupid, it's my fault for
forgetting the Pill – it's the
wrong time and the wrong
place to have a baby.

### What's going on in my heart?

I've done lots of crying - I had plans to have a baby but not like
this. I've not been drinking because I'm pregnant.
I've never been against abortion for others but I don't think I'd do it.
I feel I've let myself down and everybody else.
I feel guilty about not telling my boyfriend - not sure what this
will mean for our future.

### Support

Friends
Student services

### Me

Mind of my own.
Enjoying sister's
baby, not sure
ready for
my own

© image

**Blank 4H Tool to copy and fill your own life in:**

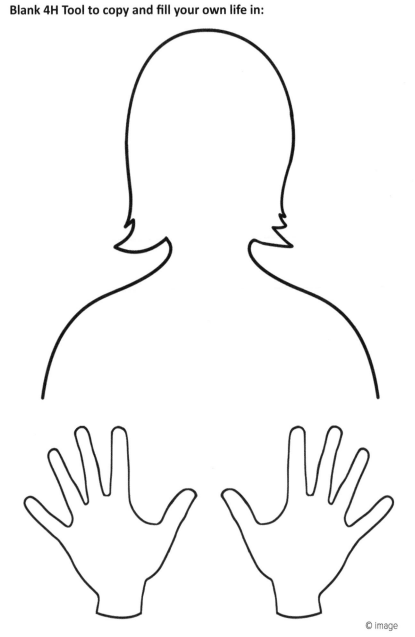

© image

Now that you have explored your thoughts, feelings and resources you are in stronger place to look at the **options**.

# Chapter 5
# Your Options

**Well done if you've made it this far!** You know more about yourself, your situation and your strengths. Now let's have a look at options. After all, no options mean no choices! We are at the second layover, 'Look at options', on the Journey to Decision picture back on page 31.

1. Looking at options
2. Weighing the gains and losses of an option
3. Making an informed decision

## 1. Looking at options

There are three main options in pregnancy: parenting, fostering/adoption or abortion.

The order in which you consider options depends on you. If you don't want to look at one of them, think about why not.

**Parenting** may be daunting, but it is still the age-old option that kept generations going. Many women tell us decades later of their satisfaction despite enormous hurdles while looking after their offspring. Most women choose this overall.

**Giving the baby** to someone else to care for is often the option that people find most difficult to consider. However, for someone who feels that they cannot parent but want to avoid abortion, then temporary fostering to gain time may be the best.

**Some countries offer safe** places in or near a hospital, often called 'baby windows', where you can leave a baby anonymously. You put the baby on a warmed cot and a bell rings to call a nurse for immediate care. A letter is there waiting for you with contact numbers for further help. The letter may say that you can change your mind in the next 12 months; if not the baby will be given to foster parents and may be adopted.

**Abortion usually** feels like the short road to relief, opening the door to carry on with life seemingly as before; yet it closes off routes to many possibilities that a new life brings – whether parented or handed to others. So, there are pros and cons to be weighed up.

## 2. Weighing the gains and losses of an option

Again, we need a simple tool to help think over the pros and cons. We are at the third layover, 'Gains and losses', on the Journey to Decision picture on page 31. This table helps you think and gives you a score at the end. The top score does not fix you on a decision – but by the time you complete the table you will know your own feelings far better.

So, take a large sheet of paper, and make a table (you can shred this soon). Draw 4 columns down it like this.

|  | Abortion | Parenting | Fostering/Adoption |
|---|---|---|---|
| My thoughts/feelings |  |  |  |
|  |  |  |  |
| Gains |  |  |  |
|  |  |  |  |
| Losses |  |  |  |
|  |  |  |  |
| Information needed |  |  |  |

© Image

Name each column with the options across the top, as shown.

As an example, look at Claire's story, the same Claire we met for the 4H Tool.

Below each entry Claire has scored her Gains and Losses out of 10 – where 10 is very important and 1 is least important.

## Options table – using Claire's thoughts as an example:

| My thoughts and feelings revealed | Abortion | Parenting | Adoption/fostering |
|---|---|---|---|
| **My thoughts and feelings revealed** | I feel it is my only choice. I can study. No need to tell Mum or Tim. Will my life go on as before? | Am I ready to parent? Can I study with a baby? Tim wants to be a father. | I always thought, not for me – but my college friends Alice and Ed are so happy they adopted. |
| **Gains** on scale 1-5 | Continue life as before 4<br>Mum won't know 2<br>Tim won't know 2<br>... ..<br>... ..<br>Total = | My own baby – wow! 5<br>Tim crazy to be a Dad 4<br>Honest with Mum 3<br>Feels lighter in my heart 3<br>... ..<br>... ..<br>Total = | Continue college 5<br>No kid to hold me back 5<br>Doing my best for baby 5<br>... ..<br>... ..<br>Total = |
| **Losses** on scale 1-5 | I can't be honest with Mum 3<br>Break trust with Tim 3<br>Losing the baby hurts 4<br>Infertile after abortion? 4<br>... ..<br>... ..<br>Total = | A kid holds back plans 4<br>Stretch marks? 2<br>Money concerns 3<br>... ..<br>... ..<br>Total = | Lose this chance of mothering 5<br>Can I cope emotionally? 4<br>Not sure how it works 2<br>... ..<br>... ..<br>Total = |
| **Information I still Need** | What chance of after-effects? Infertility risk? | Would Mum help us? How can I be OK for money? | Talk to Tim<br>See Fostering/Adoption chapter |

**The first row** asks you to consider what it would mean to you to either have an abortion, or to parent, or to choose fostering/adoption. You may have covered some of this when exploring your situation with the 4H Tool in the last chapter, so use that as a starting point.

Every choice we make balances gains and losses, pros and cons. This happens in everyday options like what to eat and what to wear, through to who we live with.

Next, you are going to give a numbered value to each gain or loss. This numbering helps you find what's in your own mind; a task that can be a challenge when one knows that making one choice means rejecting others.

On your chart, fill in the Gains and Losses for each option.

- What would you gain from abortion – what would you lose?
- What would you gain from parenting – what would you lose?
- What would you gain from fostering or adoption – what would you lose?

Now look at the lists again. Some things on the list carry more weight than others. **Underline the things** on the list that carry the most weight for you.

**Give them a score** on a scale of one to 10, where 10 is the most important.

**Total up the gains and losses** for each option. Be ready to be surprised how 'weighing' the options – while it does not bind you to a course of action – helps you *think* what you really want.

**Now do a reality check:**

- Did you list any fear that will probably never happen?
- If your situation changed, would you still be happy with your choice?

**Finally** list bits of information you still need to find on the row along the bottom. For instance, you might write,

1. What sort of abortion is done at this stage of pregnancy?

2. I don't know the side effects of abortion and I must find them in Part 2...

### 3.  Making an informed decision

To make an informed decision you need facts like you jotted down just above or on the bottom row of the chart – facts that affect you and the options you have. Most of these facts about abortion, pregnancy and adoption are in this guide; so, look at the Contents page again to find what you need.

We are at the fourth layover, 'Information', on the Journey to Decision picture on page 31. Before making final choices, pause... Give yourself time to reflect. If possible talk it through with your partner. There is still a bit more to explore and put into the decision-making.

When you are ready, go to the next chapter.

# Chapter 6
# Nearing Decision Time

**So far on the Journey to Decision** you have:

- Looked at your life now, heart values and resources.
- Explored the options and what each would mean for you.
- Noted down information still needed for informed choice.

**This chapter now covers:**

1. When to decide
2. Feelings after making the choice
3. Regrets?
4. The next steps

By now you should know what the root problem is that you face. You will be asking, 'Will abortion solve the root problem?' For instance, if the problem is to keep the pregnancy secret, then abortion seems the safe simple solution at first. But other options usually exist...

Have you considered other solutions? For instance, finding a safe house, or a Baby Window Cot ready to take a baby no questions asked, or a friendly hospital where you can give birth hidden away and be linked with social services' help? We have seen these work time and again.

What about future complications which can make abortion anything but 'simple' – like infection leading to long-term pain or infertility? (See chapter 11 'Abortion Explored'.)

## 1. When to decide

Now look over the notes you made and begin to plan which route you will take at the crossroads of decision (see picture page 31). Again, we encourage sharing this process of decision with your partner (or the father of the fetus) if possible. We realise this maybe out of the question.

There may be people to tell – friends and family. Speaking it out to someone helps you rehearse the reasons and see if you are comfortable with them.

Pregnancy decisions can be very difficult, but if you lack peace of mind with a decision, it points to that option not sitting well with you. Would another choice be more rewarding – one that keeps 'head and heart' working in harmony?

When doubts persist, go back to the 4H Tool in chapter 3 to find out why you are not at ease. You may want to revise your plans. You may need to talk it over further with somebody.

## 2.  Feelings after making the choice

One of the commonest emotions after making a pregnancy *choice* is relief, because the tension of decision-making is gone. But the feelings after deciding are not a good guide to how you will feel after the abortion is over.

For some, this relief after the decision will continue during and after an abortion, and they adjust back into life easily. But others – women and men – may feel much worse after abortion, shocked, bereaved and perhaps suicidal within days or weeks.[1]

## 3.  Regrets?

Regret is a difficult feeling to live with and will lie buried in our hearts only to pop up in unexpected ways.

People who push ahead into parenting very rarely express regret. We recently surveyed a combined 120 years of medical experience in some colleagues. Only one (in a mother-to-mother chat) had met a woman who felt her fourth child had been one too many.

Counsellors consistently report older women with anguish over past abortion – even if it had seemed easy at the time. Commonest is, 'I think of the baby every day of my life.'

When 101 women were questioned after abortion, many felt immediate relief. But this was soon followed by regret and self-blame. Three-fifths reported the abortion had a destructive impact on their intimate relationships. More than two-fifths considered suicide, and a third of the women reported at least one attempt to take their own life. All the women without exception continued to be troubled by the memory of their abortion.[2]

## 4. The next steps

First, explore the Contents page again to see what *more information* you must check out in Part 2. For instance, try the **Personal check of your mental risk** in chapter 13 'Early After-effects'.

Soon a visit to your doctor will be helpful, whatever you have decided.

There is hope and there is help. There is support available for you (see Appendix 2 'Finding Help').

# Part 2
# Exploring Your Options and Essential Facts

Choose what you need from the next chapters. They cover pregnancy dates and the changes in the fetus inside a pregnant woman. Then the question of the fetus' feelings before the main options of parenting, fostering and adoption or abortion with essential information you need to know.

Then follow the laws on abortion and the all-important after-effects of abortion – not to be missed before deciding. Rounding off Part 2 come Teenagers, Men and Pre-birth Testing.

# Chapter 7
# Week-by-week of Pregnancy

Here's a quick look at what your 'pregnancy dates' mean and what is happening in your body. If you did biology at school much is familiar, but new discoveries keep coming, such as the spark at conception.

**This chapter covers:**

1. Pregnancy dates
2. From Conception to fetus
3. Week-by-week through pregnancy
4. Life outside the womb
5. Reassurance

## 1. Pregnancy dates

Random sex just once, near a woman's mid-cycle (without contraception) makes a pregnancy on between 1 in 10 to 1 in 3 occasions.[1]

**Your pregnancy dates** are given as the number of weeks from your last menstrual period **(LMP)**. So, to work out the real age of the fetus, take away two weeks from the number of weeks since your last period.

For example, if your LMP was 1 February and today it is 28 March, you are now eight weeks pregnant 'by dates'. The true age of your embryo is 8 - 2 = 6 weeks old.

The growing human is called an *embryo* for the first eight weeks of life since conception. From eight weeks she/he is a *fetus* up to birth.[2] People call their pregnancy 'the baby' at any stage of pregnancy, depending on their thoughts about the future of the pregnancy at that moment.

## 2. From conception to fetus

Pregnancy begins in a woman's reproductive organs, see the picture below.

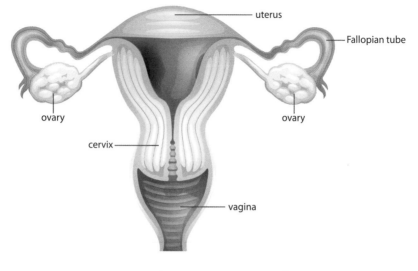

**Female reproductive organs[3]**

First, have a look for the ovary in the picture, where the eggs are stored. It is an oval the size of a small plum. Once during the monthly cycle, an egg (or ovum) is released from one of the ovaries and sucked up by the fallopian tube. Conception happens in the tube if all goes normally.

This egg travels the fallopian tube towards the uterus. Each egg can be fertilised (at conception) for some days after the woman has had sex. If not, it's lost with the blood of her monthly period.

After conception the brand-new embryo travels for up to a week down the fallopian tube, exits the tube into the womb, aiming to become attached (implanted) in the wall of the womb. That's called **implantation**.

You may see some slight bleeding at implantation. This 'show' is easily mistaken for a period, even though you are pregnant. That's one reason women fail to realise they are pregnant.

'To see the zinc spark radiate in a burst from the human egg was breathtaking,' said Professor Teresa Woodruff.[4] A bright *spark* was photographed by scientists in 2016 at a human conception. Conception is an incredible event, so complex that it is still far from fully understood.

Most incredibly, the gene code of the mother and father are combined into a new code, never known before – which became you or me – the blueprint of a full human being.

Inside the genes are all the characteristics of one person, from conception to old age. They fix the eye colour, sex, size and shape of a person packaged in the size of this dot/period here. Conception is complete in a few hours after the sperm and egg have met and mixed their genes.[5]

A positive blood test for pregnancy can be gained as early as four to five days before a missed period.[6]

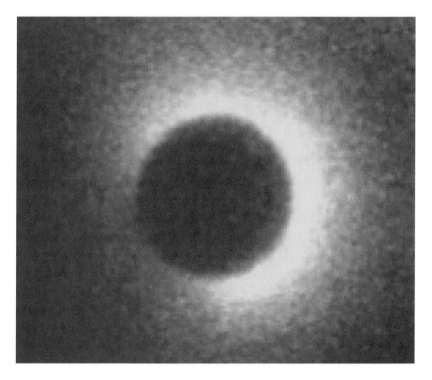

**Sparks at conception**

The flash of light when the human sperm enters the egg, never seen before April 2016.[7]

The chart below shows what is happening between conception and normal birth at around 40 weeks from the LMP week-by-week.

## 3. Week-by-week through pregnancy

| Pregnancy weeks since LMP<br>Embryo/Fetus age in weeks | Pregnancy happenings |
|---|---|
| **Weeks 1–2**<br><br>Embryo 0–1 | Ovulation happens about mid-cycle and conception is possible for a few days after. So, conception happened about 2 weeks or more after your LMP (depending on the length of your menstrual cycle).<br><br>Within hours, the embryo has messaged the woman they are there by sending out HCG hormone which begins to change her body and feelings to nurture the embryo.<br><br>The pinhead-sized embryo looks deceptively simple. Yet even the cell wall of the embryo contains about 100,000 enzymes in working harmony.<br><br>Like some sort of futuristic city, chemical messengers fly in all directions while 'builders' lay blocks with bewildering speed. Scientists are baffled by so much in this explosive growth. |
| **Weeks 2–3**<br><br>Embryo 1–3 | We are near the end of week two after your LMP and conception has just happened.<br><br>During week three after your LMP, the one-week old embryo – ballooning in size all the time – is wafted along the fallopian tube towards the womb, where it implants in the wall (implantation) on day seven.<br><br>By one-week old, the cells have multiplied 100 times. |

| | |
|---|---|
| **Week 4 from LMP**<br><br>Embryo 2 | **Most pregnancy tests** will show positive now because the embryo is pumping out the HCG that the test detects. |
| **Weeks 5–6**<br><br>Embryo 3–5 | **Division** of the two-week embryo occurs into baby and placenta.<br><br>The placenta cells reach out and link with the mother's blood supply. So far the embryo has been fed from the tiny 'yolk sac' but now the mother's blood is supplying food.<br><br>**Nerve cells** are beginning to form in the 3-week brain with spikes of activity. The basics of **major organs** are in place and the **heart** is one of the first.<br><br>**The heart begins beating** at <u>three weeks plus five days = 26 days from conception</u>. Yes, it's that accurate!<br><br>**Blood** is forming from the fourth week onwards.[8]<br><br>**Movements** can be clearly seen on ultrasound scans once the embryo is between four and six weeks old.<br><br>**Ear and eye dimples** appear on the side of the head. |
| **Week 7**<br><br>Embryo 4–6 | The developing **arms and legs** are visible swellings (limb buds).<br><br>By now the embryo is covered with a delicate layer of see-through **skin**.<br><br>**The brain** is growing fast – faster than the body. The inner **hearing** mechanism is forming, and the limb buds start to form cartilage for **bones**. |
| **Week 8**<br><br>Embryo 6 | The **jellybean-sized** human has lengthening legs, though the different parts are not so distinct yet. Soon the **knees**, ankles, thighs and **toes** develop. |

| | |
|---|---|
| **Week 9**<br><br>Embryo 7 | **The face** is slowly forming. The eyes are bigger and more obvious with some colour.<br><br>There is a **mouth and tongue**, complete with tiny taste buds.<br><br>**Major organs** such as the heart, brain, lungs, kidneys and gut are being formed and filled. **Fingerprints** are being engraved permanently.<br><br>From now on, the embryo is called a fetus (meaning 'offspring'). |
| **Week 10**<br><br>Fetus 8 | Small, jerky **movements** are there on the ultrasound scan and the **heart** is tapping out 180 beats a minute, audible on the scan if the volume is turned up.<br><br>Two tiny nostrils are visible. |
| **Week 11**<br><br>Fetus 9 | Growth spurts ahead and the bones of the face are now formed with a jaw bone and full set of milk teeth.<br><br>A nose is appearing.<br><br>The eyelids remain closed and won't open for a few months.<br><br>The ear buds begin to resemble ears as they grow.<br><br>The head makes up one-third of the fetus' length, but the body is growing fast and straightening.<br><br>The fingers and toes are separating, and fingernails appearing.<br><br>Antenatal clinics do a **dating ultra-sound scan** at 11–14 weeks after LMP. The age of the fetus is given in weeks from the LMP.<br><br>Abortion clinics also do dating scans.<br><br>The midwife can work out the **expected date of delivery (EDD)**. |

| | |
|---|---|
| **Week 12**<br><br>Fetus 10 | The fetus is now **fully formed**. All the organs, muscles, limbs and bones are in place, and the sex organs present.<br><br>From now on, it's about growing and maturing. Although the fetus is moving quite a lot, it's too early for the mother to feel those movements but she will soon. The skeleton is soft cartilage, beginning to harden into bone.<br><br>**Pain**, such as needle pricks from a doctor, make the fetus pull away. |
| **Week 13**<br><br>Fetus 11 | External **sex organs** are appearing as a swelling between the legs while the **ovaries or testes** are fully developed inside the body in line with their female XX or male XY gene blue-print. |
| **Week 14**<br><br>Fetus 12 | **Twin pregnancies** are bonding through touching in the womb at 14 weeks.[9] They are about the length of a man's finger (ten centimetres) from head to bottom curled up.<br><br>About now the fetus begins **swallowing** small amounts of the fluid it swims in. The **kidneys** clean the baby's blood making **urine**, which passes back into the amniotic fluid. |
| **Week 15**<br><br>Fetus 13 | They will be hearing their **mother's voice**, heartbeat, digestive gurgles and dim sounds from the world outside.<br><br>The **eyes** detect light and though closed can be aware of a bright light shone through the tummy.<br><br>**Pain sensations** are not only fully developed but seem to be *hypersensitive* from perhaps 15 weeks onwards. (See next chapter.) |
| **Week 16**<br><br>Fetus 14 | The fetus begins **making facial expressions**. The **hands** can reach, hold each other and form a fist. |

| Weeks 17–19 Fetus 15–17 | The fetus is moving around lots and may respond to music or other loud noises from outside. |
|---|---|
| | The fetus is growing bigger and the head and body are more in proportion. The face is looking more like a child, with eyebrows and eyelashes. The eyes are moving, although the eyelids remain closed. |
| | The mouth can now open and close. The fingerprints are established with their identity. |
| | In the UK, the NHS offers a **high-definition ultrasound scan** between 18 and 21 weeks; this examines the body. Even when done with care, the results can reassure that all is well when it is not, or mistakenly advise that something is wrong before the child arrives fully healthy. (See chapter 17, 'Disability and Pre-birth Tests'.) |
| | **Babies born** from this stage on may survive with breathing efforts for some hours, but even with intensive care, they cannot live long. |
| | During surgery on the fetus – such as to repair spina bifida – British anaesthetists now give the fetus pain relief from 18 weeks.[10] |

| | |
|---|---|
| **Weeks 20–24**<br><br>Fetus 18–22 | **Babies born** from around the start of this stage on may survive for some hours, but even with intensive care, they cannot live long.<br><br>Fine soft hair covers the body and they begin a sleeping waking pattern, which may be different from the mother's.<br><br>The lungs are not yet able to function properly, but the fetus is practising breathing actions.<br><br>**Premature babies** born at 22 weeks, weighing just 1lb or 500g, now have a reasonable chance of survival with intensive care.<br><br>However, while survival is certainly possible, there is a significant risk of long-term disability. (See chapter 20 'Premature Birth After Abortion'.)<br><br>A baby born at 24 weeks has a better chance of a healthy future than at 22 weeks.<br><br>As a doctor treating new-borns, I was happy if a baby stayed inside mum until at least 28 weeks, because I knew they usually romp into childhood. (Note: evidence suggests that even babies born at 34–37 weeks have a risk of early and long-term complications.)[11] |
| **Weeks 25–28**<br><br>Fetus 23–26 | Somersaulting and lively actions are filmed on scans and reported by mothers, including responses to **sound and touch**.<br><br>The eyelids open for the first time and soon start blinking.<br><br>The brain, lungs and digestive system are completely formed now but need time to become fully functional. By 28 weeks the fetus is formed and functioning.<br><br>As said, **pain sensations** seem to be *hypersensitive* from perhaps 15 weeks onwards. (See next chapter.) |

| Weeks 29–32 Fetus 27–30 | The skin is getting less wrinkled as they **put on weight**. The fetus is thumb-sucking and able to focus their eyes on objects. |
|---|---|
| Weeks 33–36 Fetus 31–33 | **The bones** are hardening, apart from the skull bones, which stay separated and soft so birth can happen. At 33 weeks the brain and nervous system are completely developed, and at 36 weeks the lungs are fully mature. |
| Weeks 37–birth Fetus 35–39 | The pregnancy is called full-term at 37 weeks from the LMP. All being well, the fetus' head moves down into the pelvis about now, beginning their journey of birth. The average British baby weighs 7lbs 8oz (3.4 kg) at birth. |

Watch the video on The Endowment for Human Development website.[12]

## 4. Life outside the womb

Babies born too early have survival rates in Sweden of:

- At 22 weeks over 1 in 2 (60%)
- At 23 weeks, 2 in 3 (70%)
- At 26 weeks 9 out of 10 survive (90%)

The UK and Holland neonatologists usually try to resuscitate from 23 weeks, Sweden from 22 weeks. Survival once these extremely pre-term children are born is easier to predict when they have had three weeks of intensive care.[13]

Babies as young as seven months can choose between good and bad, right and wrong.[14]

## 5. Reassurance

Most women manage pregnancy well and deliver their baby fine, despite the physical and emotional changes that pregnancy brings.

# Chapter 8
# Feelings of a Fetus

**This chapter covers:**

1. Does the fetus suffer?
2. The evidence
3. Perinatal hospice for the fetus to die in comfort
4. Conclusions and actions for you

## 1. Does the fetus suffer?

Naturally women ask, 'Does my fetus suffer during abortion?' Pain relief for the fetus is not routinely offered at abortion – does it matter? After all, any of us can think, 'During abortion the little thing will never know anything – so it doesn't matter.' But the first problem is that any anaesthetic pain relief given to the woman will not reach her unborn.[1]

So, what does the young human feel? As neonatologist Dr Robin Pierucci MD said, 'Every parent knows babies feel pain... except when it's called a fetus.'[2] The UK Department of Health now recommends help to the fetus for pain from 20 weeks and older. (They suddenly changed because fetal surgery for spina bifida arrived in the UK.)[3]

Nevertheless, people still argue babies can't feel pain and in fact doctors did not give anaesthetic to new-borns having surgery until the 1990s. Abortion surgeons have been much slower to catch up with anaesthetic for the fetus – so far.

**In brief** yes, the fetus feels pain as young as 15 weeks. However, the arguments bounce back and forwards about when suffering and pain is felt beyond 15 weeks.

At abortion, you can take steps to relieve suffering in your fetus by insisting on proper pain relief for them before the event, or realising their pain cannot be relieved and refusing to abort out of compassion.

## 2. The evidence

Videos show the fetus pulling back from needles from around 12 weeks old. Doctors can see a fetus holding the needle in its body at 15 weeks.[4] Current opinion is that a fetus can feel pain in the way you or I can from between 20 and 24 weeks,[5] but British anaesthetists give pain relief from 18 weeks for fetal surgery 'to be sure', and others say it may be from 15 weeks and a fetus is more, not less, pain sensitive, saying they are 'extremely sensitive to painful stimuli'.[6]

The table shows the abortion procedures where fetal pain could be an issue: a mid to late second trimester dilation and evacuation (D&E) procedure and a third trimester lethal injection (feticide).

During the D&E procedure, according to the RCOG, the 'fetus is removed in fragments', a so-called 'dismemberment' abortion; each limb is removed, then 'crushing an infant's skull'[7] allowing the torso to be pulled out.[8]

In Britain, older fetuses at abortion get an injection of potassium chloride to stop the beating heart – it takes from minutes up to **several hours** to work according to the British Pregnancy Advisory Service who do them.[9] Potassium Chloride injections in adults cause severe burning pain.

Either of these procedures – the dismemberment or the injection – would be excruciatingly painful in an adult, however, they would be more painful at these ages because of 'hypersensitivity' (they are feeling pain four times as strongly).[10] In fact, the ability to dull pain – the pain inhibitory pathways – doesn't develop until around 40 weeks. **Hence, prior to either of these procedures, an opioid painkiller such as fentanyl is essential.**

A jumping fetus might be felt by the mother and also evade the needle. So, some try and inject a muscle-paralysing drug to stop the fetus jumping in pain and to dampen the potential feelings the woman may experience.

British anaesthetists may sometimes give the baby fentanyl – a powerful painkiller – immediately before the lethal injection, but it is not yet standard policy.

**Action point:** Be sure to insist on fentanyl for your fetus, because it is unclear in the UK what age fentanyl is given. Nevertheless the evidence that analgesia confers any benefit on the fetus at any gestation is lacking.[11]

## The milestones in fetal feelings

| Fetal Age | 4-7 | 8-11 | 12-15 | 16-19 | 20-23 | 24-27 | 28-31 | 32-35 | 36-39 | 40+ |
|---|---|---|---|---|---|---|---|---|---|---|
| Method of Abortion: | Medical | | Suction Aspiration | Dilation and Evacuation | | | Labour & Delivery -either whole or in pieces / Lethal injection of potassium chloride into heart | | | |
| Fetal Activities from this stage onwards: | Heart begins to beat at 18 days | Kicking, stretching, fingers open/close, toes curl | Moving facial muscles, sucking thumb, sensing light | Swallowing, full on kicks, mother may notice patterns in activity | Sounds remembered and recognised | Exhaling/inhaling fluid, regular wake/sleep pattern, blinking | Turning head from side to side | Activity as newborn | Activity as newborn | Activity as newborn |
| Fetal Pain Milestones | | (Recoiling reflexes to noxious stimuli) | Spinal cord/Thalamus connections begin (14 weeks); lower brain pain perception possible. | Spinal cord/Thalamus connections complete (18 weeks). Advanced physiological response to painful stimuli. Brain signals begin. | Brain signal patterns mature | Thalamus fully connected to cortex (higher brain pain perception now possible) | | | | Pain inhibitory pathways develop |

thalamic pain perception

cortical pain perception

Dr Robin Pierucci's advice is, 'Given the recent changes by paediatricians to recognise a new-born's need of pain relief, laws should enforce this for the unborn also.'[12]

Officially, for late abortions England and Wales recorded 252 done at 24 weeks or older in 2017, but others happen illegally, on request, over the age of 30 weeks as we have personally seen in England. Some 'legal' late abortions were for minor problems like cleft palate, which can be easily corrected by surgery; others were for spina bifida (which can now be corrected by surgery on the fetus before birth). Down's syndrome and chromosome problems were the largest group, accounting for a third of late abortions.[13]

## 3. Perinatal hospice for the fetus to die in comfort

For a fetus with brief life expectancy, due to a heart or brain condition that is expected to end their life within hours, abortion is often offered or heavily recommended to parents. There is a better way for these distressing cases. (For the effect on parents, see chapter 17 'Disability and Pre-birth Tests'.)

First, note that late abortion for major disability is not usually needed for a safe delivery.[14] Infants with a large head can be delivered by caesarean section (C-section).

In perinatal care (meaning just before and after birth), the aim is that the mother can deliver and hold her baby peacefully and – if alive – let her or him die naturally and grieve naturally. Perinatal hospice (www.Perinatalhospice. org) has been pioneered in the United States to do this. People interviewed reported 60% to 80% wanting this route rather than abortion.[15]

**Anencephaly** is a distressing problem, where the baby has a face but is missing most of the brain behind, as in this photo.[16] They tend to live for a few hours only after birth. Most medics were trained to believe they were 'brain dead'.

Yet, anencephalic babies can:[17]

- React to pain
- Be soothed by a cuddle
- Show wake and sleep cycles

**Baby with anencephaly**

This illustrates how pleasure and pain are more complex than believed, whether brain or partial brain is present, and arguments that the fetus does not feel should be balanced against the evidence that they do.

In 2017, England and Wales did 3,314 abortions due to the risk that the child would be born seriously handicapped. That is under Ground E of the Abortion Act (see also chapter 12 'Abortion Law'.)[18]

## 4. Conclusions and actions for you

Humane pain relief for the fetus in abortion has not caught up with rapid progress to relieve fetal suffering in the last 20 years. So, the unborn may suffer during abortion. You can insist on pain relief for the fetus during abortion, but it is technically hard for a doctor to achieve it for a fetus younger than 15 or 20 weeks.

# Chapter 9
# Parenting Explored

This chapter covers:

1. Looking at my circumstances now
2. Can I cope?
3. What help is available to me?
4. What next?

---

**Evelyn's story**

When my GP gave me the news that I was over 14 weeks pregnant, I couldn't sleep. Yes, I had missed some periods recently, but I explained them away with change of country and stress.

My mind was full of thoughts. How did I miss the early pregnancy? What was happening to my body? How could I adapt to become a mum? I knew it would change my life forever.

I found my partner Pete and asked him: 'Would I be able to look after my baby in good times and in bad? What if things were not all normal with the baby? What if I couldn't cope? What about my job and my career plans?'

'Pete, are you ready to start a family?' Would we both be willing to give up our freedom, our peaceful nights and our energy?

I was overwhelmed. I felt weak and quite sick at the sheer thought of it all.

---

This story shows the shock that an unexpected pregnancy can bring and some of the issues involved when thinking about parenting.

It may be difficult, for several reasons, to think about continuing the pregnancy and having a baby. This chapter helps you look at this option realistically.

**Eleanor's story**

When I fell pregnant, I loathed myself and I wished the baby dead. I felt so sick I could die myself.

But once I'd seen Jimmy on the scan – loathing slowly became 'I love you!' His birth changed my life, and every day varies.

I'm dog-tired, but I still enjoy watching him explore... and watching him asleep is even better!

Breastfeeding went from panic to peace. Thank you, Jimmy, for making me a mother.

## 1. Looking at my circumstances now

Parenting has been the heart's desire of most people since time began. Scary? Maybe... or maybe joyful. Can it be done? There may be no easy answers to the situation you are in. Yet, family doctors hear amazing stories of women who find inner resources to rear their children.

Here are some fears and concerns in common situations:

- **It may be to do with the father**

  It may be that you don't want to go on to parent because you don't want to be connected to the person who is the father of the baby. He may be abusive, or you just don't want to be with him, or you can't be with him for various reasons.

  It may help to separate out two questions you're faced with:

  a. *Is it to do with the man I am partnered with, or perhaps the man who fathered the fetus?*

    The answer to this may be a clear 'no' or it may be, 'I would carry on with him if I could' and carry some heartache with it. Coming to terms with your future relationship with him is important.

  b. *Is it about having the baby?*

Am I able to love and care for this child on my own? Is there a way it could work? What role will the father play? Is it possible to break the relationship and continue the pregnancy? What do I need to consider?

- **It may be to do with other people knowing**

  Maybe you don't want to continue the pregnancy because there is someone who you feel should not know about it. This could be your parent(s), school, work, community, or your partner, especially if the pregnancy is from someone else.

  A trained counsellor can help you explore how to move forward. Keeping a secret like this can be overwhelming and exhausting. Being able to share it with someone outside your situation may be the most helpful way of thinking it through.

  Getting to a safe and secret location may be needed. Across the world, life centres and some hospitals have ways of helping pregnant women kindly and discretely.

- **Something may be wrong with the baby**

  Perhaps you are feeling you could not face parenting if there was a disability. Some recent test result or worries about medication you have taken may be causing you concern.

  You can check out the effects of any medication on the developing fetus by looking online at www.medicines.org.uk, and you could talk through the implications of this with a professional (see Appendix 2 'Finding Help').

  No one can give assurances that your baby will be born perfect, and 'disability' can cover a very wide range of issues, from very mild problems like cleft palate to major problems like spina bifida. All these can be helped in some ways.

  Exploring exactly what you have been told, how accurate a diagnosis you have, and all the fears that come with that, is the next step. Any mention of disability in the fetus can bring on panic, so it is important to have time and space to think through any implications before deciding. (More on this in chapter 17, 'Disability and Pre-birth Tests'.)

- **It may be to do with the timing**

  Maybe you are feeling this is the wrong time to have a baby: you may
  be in the middle of studying; you may have just started a job or got a
  promotion recently; you may already have the number of children you
  want; you may feel like you have not had a chance to do the things you
  want to do.

  Any parent will agree there is a cost to parenting – physically,
  emotionally, financially, as well as in time and commitment. You will
  need to weigh up which of the things you would be sacrificing *now*
  can be picked up later, and which ones you could continue with a
  child.

## 2. Can I cope?

At this point, we suggest going back to your notes from Part 1 'The Journey
to a Decision'. Look back at your gains and losses for parenting and how
you rated them. If you did not complete that exercise, do it now.

Go back to the 4H Tool and look again at what you are bringing into the
situation. Ask yourself:

- **What internal resources and strengths do I have?**

  What personal qualities do I have that would help me to parent? What
  personal qualities might stop me parenting well? What could I put in
  place to equip me if I'm struggling?

## 3. What help is available to me?

Who is willing to step in and give me a hand? Is my partner up for it? Can
my parents assist? What about my friends? Are there any agencies out
there that could support me if I decide to continue the pregnancy? How
could they help?

Whilst parenting can bring much love and joy into your life, there are also
challenges. Raising a child can put pressure on your finances, your time
and on your relationships, and it can affect your freedom, your work or
studies.

Information is available from your local council, church, health service and local government or organisations like Citizens Advice in the UK.

If you have a pregnancy centre in your area, they may be able to help you with the information you need and provide you with practical support.

**The Internet** offers local information, and there are some websites below for help in the UK you may find useful as well as in Appendix 2 'Finding Help'.

- **Finances**

  Visit the NHS website[1] for information about benefits and housing you can claim when you are pregnant or have a child.

  **Asylum seekers** can find out more about the help available to them on the government website.[2]

  **Students** can visit the NHS website which lists the benefits you're entitled to when you're pregnant, and has information on maternity, paternity and shared parental leave.[3]

  Non-English speakers will often find translators available.

- **Healthcare**

  Once you have registered with a local GP in the UK, all are entitled to free antenatal health care (www.maternityaction.org.uk/ explains entitlement for asylum seekers).

- **Housing**

  If you have housing needs, you can contact the Housing Department of your local council for housing advice. See also the websites for Shelter[4] and Life[5].

- **Education**

  It is usually possible to continue with your education while pregnant. If you are under 16, the local authority has a legal requirement to provide you with education. How this happens varies across regions and schools. For more information visit the BabyCentre website.[6]

If you are a student under 20, you may be eligible for childcare costs under Care to Learn.[7] You must be aged under 20 at the start of your course.

Juggling study and being a parent, whilst extremely rewarding, can also be a real struggle. The NUS (National Union of Students) is working to make a fairer system for all student parents.[8]

• **Single parents**

Support is available through Gingerbread[9] and, if you are having problems with isolation, through Home-Start.[10]

The local crisis pregnancy centre or a Life centre (google 'life pregnancy centres near me') offer baby clothes and equipment, as well as emotional support throughout your pregnancy. Children's centres help from birth to 5 years.[11]

## 4. What next?

Now that you've had a chance to consider some of the issues and help available around parenting, spend some time imagining yourself as a mum. Despite challenges, most mothers look back on parenting as a positive experience. Many call it a privilege to bring up a child as best as they can despite sacrifices.

# Chapter 10
# Fostering and Adoption Explored

What do John Lennon, Bill Clinton and Nelson Mandela have in common? Adopting parents shaped their destinies.[1]

Thinking about giving your baby to someone else to care for takes courage but opens doors beyond imagination.

Some people in our writing team have experience in fostering and adoption; we know its potential and the challenges.

I knew women say before birth, 'If I had the baby – then I'd want to keep him. So, doctor, I want an abortion.'

I've never known a woman to say, 'I wish I'd never had this baby,' but at times they may feel that way.

**This chapter covers:**

1. Why think about fostering and adoption?
2. Three main ways
3. What happens in adoption?
4. Regrets?
5. What contact can I have?
6. The numbers
7. What now?

## 1. Why think about fostering and adoption?

Here are a few examples:

- The mother doesn't agree with abortion but reckons she cannot cope with parenting given her circumstances.
- The mother risks rejection from her community as a single parent.
- The baby could be in danger from others if staying with the parent.
- The mother chooses what she considers a 'better life' for her child.

## 2. Three main ways:

- Fostering
- Special guardianship
- Adoption

**Fostering** is a way of providing children with care in a nurturing environment during a time when the family is unable to look after them. So, this is an option for the birth mother who is not yet sure what's best. The foster family cares while you think it over.

> 'If you can help a child, you don't have to spend years repairing an adult.'[2]

**Special guardianship** is a longer-term British option where parental duties are shared until the child is 18 and the mother can often have contact.

**Adoption** means giving your child to adoptive parents for good. It provides a child with a permanent home because living with their biological family is not possible. The routes are typically via social services or an independent adoption agency (see the end of this chapter and at the back of the book).

> **Adoption is a brave**, generous decision that usually brings joy to adopters and gives the child a chance of life.'
>
> Dr Kirsty Saunders, MBChB, DCH, Adoption Paediatrician

Some parents want to keep their baby, but the local social authority does not feel it is safe for the child, and this leads to 'enforced adoption'. However, the focus of this chapter is with those who are considering adoption as a choice.

> **Dominic** has fetal alcohol syndrome which can impair mental function. His adoptive parents Ron and Avril say, 'Since adopting Dominic, he is just so happy, always happy. Dominic is very intelligent. You can feel quite chuffed you have given a child a chance of life that maybe they wouldn't have had.'[3]

## 3. What happens in adoption?

There are many people waiting to adopt a baby after a rigorous screening process. You will be able to discuss the kind of family you want your child to be placed in.

Preparations for the adoption can begin before your child is born, but no permanent arrangements will be made until after you have given birth. Even then, you will be completely free to change your mind. However, once an adoption order has been made (when your child has been with their new family for a minimum of ten weeks), it cannot be changed.

The process has four stages in the UK with similarities worldwide. There is plenty of time for you to rethink and change your mind.

- A social worker will talk to you about adoption and provide initial counselling. You can request the kind of parents you would like for your baby. Agencies try to place your baby with adopting parents of your preferred ethnicity, but there is an ongoing shortage of minority families seeking to adopt. Interracial adoption is on the rise.[4]
- Immediately after the birth, you can spend some time with the baby if you want to. If you are very likely to want adoption, the baby would be placed with adopters from the beginning, but you can still see the baby and still change your mind. The baby will be placed with foster parents for at least six weeks, during which time you can visit.
- The baby is then placed with the adopting parents and, after three months, the adoption order will be applied for.
- You will then be asked by the social worker to sign a legal document and the court will make an adoption order. You are not required to attend court, but after this point you cannot change your mind.

The Adoption and Children Act 2002 (England and Wales), which came into force in September 2005, brought about several changes to adoption. Some of these changes affect the process of adoption:

- The Local Authority will look at the family of the birth father, if he has been identified. If the birth mother objects strongly, her reasons for objection will be investigated. However, the father has a say in the decision if he has parental responsibility (that means he is named on the birth certificate or he is married to you as the birth mother).

## 4. Regrets?

During decades of work as medical professionals, we were humbled by the courage and willingness of mothers with an unwanted pregnancy to give their child for adoption. I cannot remember any with serious regrets, but this is not to say it never happens.

You may be wondering if you might regret adoption. Susan Rose, founder of Fetal Alcohol Syndrome Network of New York City has said, 'This is an extremely tough question to answer. My husband has said repeatedly: 'If I knew then what I know now... NO!' Yet, I've never seen a better father... ever.'[5] And another view is in the following box.

---

'Our adopted daughter gave us hell for the first thirteen years. Then she changed into a wonderful person.

Recently I saw a picture of her wedding with her birth mother standing beside her. It was only illness that prevented me from attending.'

Mrs X, 2018, UK

---

We suggest glancing back now to your own Head and Heart thinking we did in chapter 4. None of us can predict our future nor avoid every regret in life. But by counting the cost now on each option, you will have less cause for regret ahead and more hopes of a satisfied life.

## 5. What contact can I have?

The birth mother is encouraged to write a letter to be read when the child is older, so she can explain to the child why this step was taken. Sometimes a photo of the mother with the baby is given to him or her to keep.

---

**John's mother** gave birth to him in South America and he now lives in Europe. She says, 'Knowing he was well has helped to heal the wounds.'

She could accept the decision and solution. She keeps in touch via a trusted contact person. John sends his birth mum a picture every birthday to show how he is doing.

John says, 'I did find it strange to find I had parents from South America and it was emotional to meet my mum, but well worth it.'

John, aged 19

---

You will have an opportunity to prepare a 'Life Story' book with photos that will be shared with your child by the adopting parents. There is almost always an opportunity for letter-box contact at a specified time every year, which happens through the adoption agency or through the local authority.

So, as the birth mother this means you will receive an update on your child's progress; you can respond by placing a letter on file which may or may not be shared with the child, but it is there should your child want to look when they are 18. If you want future contact with the child, you must register an interest in being found by your child.

One adoption professional says she knows of several babies adopted from birth who later have good relationships with their birth parents. Also, the birth parent and adopting parents can end up having a good relationship, like an extended family.[6]

This table compares similarities in what adoption and abortion offer you.

**SIMILARITIES**

| ADOPTION | ABORTION |
|---|---|
| You can pursue the goals you had. | You can pursue the goals you had. |
| You can live independently. | You can live independently. |
| You won't have to parent before you are ready. | You won't have to parent before you are ready. |
| Free to choose the long-term relationship with the father. | Free to choose the long-term relationship with the father. |
| You can resume your education or career. | You can resume your education or career. |

But crucial differences must be weighed up as well.

**DIFFERENCES**

| ADOPTION | ABORTION |
|---|---|
| Gives time to plan the future of your baby. | It can never be reversed. |
| You can hold and name your baby. | You cannot hold or know your baby. |
| You can continue contact with your child. | You will never see your child grow up. |
| You can feel good about your choice. | You may feel guilt or shame about your choice. |
| Your pregnancy gives life. | 'Abortion is final, adoption is a new beginning.'[7] |

## 6. The numbers

- Some sources estimate there are about 2 million couples waiting to adopt in the United States.[8]
- Creating a Family[9] has stats on numbers, waiting times and costs for the USA and other countries.
- In England, in the year ending 31 March 2018, approved adoptive parents waiting for children numbered 3,350. The number of looked after children continues to increase.[10]

## 7. What now?

If you decide that the right choice for you and your baby is adoption, you have nothing to be ashamed of – it can be a key, opening doors to many possibilities. It sets you free to carry on with your life knowing your child has a future and a hope. And for the child, they are granted the chance of the growing freedom to make their own choices in life from a safe foundation.

The downsides for the birth mum (and father and other family) are the physical and emotional costs of carrying a baby to term and perhaps giving them up – although by then mums may discover that the problems have been dealt with, things such as studies, career or inconvenient timing.

The upsides are the lifelong physical and emotional benefits of a full-term pregnancy (see chapters 13 and 14 on 'After-effects') and the heartfelt benefits of knowing you did your best for your child in the circumstances. While women may also say abortion was best for their child the evidence for high risks of emotional and physical after-effects in the woman who owned the fetus is overwhelming (see next chapters).[11]

You are entitled to counselling throughout, and time to work through the emotions. Local authorities in the UK are good at providing this.

Choosing adoption is positive for your baby's future – full of hope and potential – but, as with all pregnancy decisions, there are emotions attached to the choice you make.

Talk to experts, family and trusted friends about your thoughts on this subject. Time is on your side. Rushing will not help, so use this time wisely for a decision which will give you peace of mind for now and the long term.

More help is available in 'Finding Help' at the back of this guide.

---

**Barbara** never knew her father.

Her mum left her as a four-year-old in a children's home. 'I had a good life. We had fun and I became a midwife, which I think is ironic, since I wasn't really wanted as a baby! I'm glad I was not aborted.'

---

# Chapter 11
## Abortion Explored

The knowledge you gain in this chapter will help you to make an informed decision you feel comfortable with.

Having thought about your pregnancy in Part 1, you are in a better position to explore this option and compare abortion with parenting and adoption.

As you read on, keep in mind your main personal issues about this pregnancy, the ones that Part 1 helped you identify. Perhaps look at your notes again.

Keep asking yourself, *'Will abortion be a better, safer solution for my underlying challenge which this pregnancy has put the spotlight on?*

*In my own case, I think my underlying challenge is* _____
_____.' Write your own problem in that blank space; it could be one like these:

- *My parent(s) will go mad at me.*
- *My partner is pushing me to abort.*
- *I will lose my job.*
- *I'm 14 and will have to drop out of school.*
- *I can't give this child a home.*
- *It will cost too much money.*
- *I am anxious though I don't know why.*
- *I could lose my friends.*
- *I won't be a good mother.*
- *My partner abused me and I am scared.*

**Problems have solutions, as the contributors to this book have seen:**

- The parents of pregnant daughters usually turn into loving grandparents.
- A partner became a supportive dad.
- The woman who feared losing her job found shift-work and a nursery for her child.

- It was a struggle for the 14-year-old, but she gave birth at 15 and stayed at school to gain qualifications that led to the job she is still in now.
- In financial stress the local charity gave nappies and baby equipment. The council paid for housing.
- The anxious one felt better for a good talk to her family and social worker.
- The woman fearing she'd lose friends kept her *real* friends and made more friends at a group for mothers and babies at a local church.
- The woman unable to give her child a home arranged adoption by an infertile couple; they gave her son a loving home.
- The woman who worried about being a good mother was amazed by how well she coped.
- The woman abused considered abortion after the rape; but then said that the baby had done nothing wrong. Instead she asked her doctor to help explore some other options.

As we saw in Part 1, no one can wind back the clock or undo the pregnancy. The future will open as you find solutions for the underlying problem.

**This chapter covers:**

1. Basics
2. Complications
3. Clinic or home?
4. Medical (Chemical) methods
5. What method and when?
6. Abortion Pill Reversal
7. Surgical methods
8. Professionals involved
9. Disposal and grieving
10. After-care
11. Summary

## 1. Basics

Abortion is a major event in a woman's life. It will usually have an impact not only on her reproductive organs but also her emotions, mind and spirit.

It is the removal of a pregnancy – fetus – from the womb by chemical drugs, surgical destruction or a combination of both.

Commonly women seek to end pregnancy at around 12 weeks, so this guide majors on those situations.

**Terms people use:** the list here all mean the same end result, the end of the pregnancy.

• **Induced abortion** (IA)
• **Termination of pregnancy** (TOP)
• **Suction termination of pregnancy** (STOP)
• **Early medical abortion** (EMA).
• **Manual Vacuum Aspiration** (MVA)
• **Surgical Evacuation**

**Medical abortion** is also called **chemical abortion** or the **abortion pill**.

'**Late-term abortion**' has come to mean happening later in pregnancy, from 20 weeks up to birth. (*Medically* speaking it means from 37 weeks or older.)

**Partial birth abortion** means the baby's life is intentionally ended during birth.

**Miscarriage**, also called '**spontaneous abortion**', is the natural loss of the pregnancy before the fetus can survive independently. In most cases the cause is unknown, and the after-effects – physical and mental – are milder than after induced abortion. However, the *loss* may feel massive, so proper grieving is important. Help for any pregnancy loss is accessible through most counselling centres in Appendix 2 'Finding Help' at the end of the guide.

## 2. Complications

This large subject is introduced by Laila's true story. Full details are in chapters 13 and 14 on Early and Later After-effects.

### Laila's story

Laila was 18 and came to the hospital for an abortion during her 12th week of pregnancy. She expected to stay in hospital one day and told me the real reason for the abortion was she had a holiday booked.

She and our gynaecology boss instructed the team to say to the parents, 'She needs a D&C (Dilation & Curettage or "scrape" of her womb) for heavy periods.'

A routine abortion like Laila's means forcing open the cervix which is tightly shut to protect the fetus inside. So, the surgeon must overcome nature to force it to open.

Afterwards Laila was bleeding heavily so she was kept in hospital and given hormones to stop the bleeding – unsuccessfully.

By day three, we had created a web of lies to her parents about the so called 'D&C'. Laila lay in bed, face to the wall, saying nothing.

By day five she had had two more scrapes, and it was ten days before she could go home. The scrapes raised her risk of infections and other complications.[1]

Laila's story helps us beware of claims that, 'abortion is very safe nowadays' when not 'back-street'. At least 1 in 10 women get physical complications at abortion or a few weeks later. Infection risk is frequent (1 in 10 abortions) and this may itself cause serious bleeding, pain and collapse early on. A case was told to us this week.[2]

**Abortion Pill** adverse events (that's medical abortion) are about four times higher than surgical abortion, affecting about 1 in 5 women, but 5.6% after surgical.[3]

Serious risks were known over 2000 years ago, which is partly why doctors outlawed it. Modern doctors may still swear the Hippocratic Oath at graduation, 'I will not give to a woman a pessary to cause abortion.'

Modern research shows that many women who have received an abortion can suffer and even die long after the procedure but connected with it.

(See the 'After-effects' chapters 13 and 14.) It must be stated again that abortion is a serious procedure requiring careful choices.

**Multiple abortions** multiply several risks, including premature birth of the next baby – risks double after each abortion.

## 3. Clinic or home?

Having an abortion in a clinic is the safer option, but unsuitable premises could raise the risk of infection. It is becoming easier to obtain drugs online and abort at home, however this is risky and is not advised.

In the UK, most abortions take place in private clinics, paid for by the NHS. Some are done in NHS hospitals. You may be seen by your GP or family planning clinic then referred to an abortion clinic.

**Minimum standards:** check for these *minimum* standards to lessen your risks but remember – the best staff and facilities cannot prevent the infections and other serious after-effects.

Beware one-stop-shops offering 'counselling' and procedure on the same day. 'No other gynaecological procedure like this would happen that way.'[4]

- **Information** should be written and verbal mentioning all side-effects – even rarities.[5]
- **Counselling beforehand** is law in many countries and US states, but clinic staff struggle to find time.
- **Premises** and **staff training** should be quality checked by independent inspectors.
- **Blood tests** must be offered for Rhesus disease, possible blood transfusion and detecting STIs (sexually transmitted infections).
- **Ultrasound scan** must be done to assess the accurate age of the fetus and decide the method. This helps the clinic prove they were within the legal age limit of the pregnancy. You and your personal doctor may be refused sight of your scan where illegal dates were used and because seeing the fetus prompts you to change your mind in about 1 in 5 women. Some counsellors offer a free scan as part of holistic care, ask them or search online for your nearest scan.

- **Consent form**. As for any surgical intervention, you need to take time to inform yourself well about the procedure. It is unsafe to sign quickly, as you may regret it. Before you sign the consent form we highly recommend reading Part 1 and other relevant chapters in Part 2 of this guide.
- **You can change your mind** after signing the consent form. Women walk out of the operating room at the last minute. Information and support should be offered if you decide not to abort.[6]

## 4. Medical (Chemical) methods

'Medical' means chemically induced ejection of the pregnancy using drugs swallowed or placed in the vagina as a pessary. The combination of Mifepristone (RU-486 or Mifeprex) plus Misoprostol is usual, or Misoprostol alone.

The early **side-effects** of 'pill abortion' are very common and several times more common than surgical – affecting about one woman in 5 (1 in 20 for surgical). These are nausea, vomiting, severe stomach pain. For example, in 2005, four American women died linked to infection after medical abortion. Bleeding, ectopic pregnancy and burst uterus are familiar to people working in OB/GYN.[7] The older the fetus the greater the risk.[8]

People who survived to be born after Misoprostol have a high association with Mobius syndrome – permanent facial paralysis – as seen in Brazil.[9]

A little over half of all abortions in England and Wales[10] are done medically, despite evidence for the higher risks to women and 1 in 20 needing to be finished with surgery.[11] In Canada, only 3% happen this way.

Women may prefer the 'abortion pill' feeling it's more natural and can be used at home. Avoiding instruments can feel kinder. But the woman can experience more painful contractions compared to a surgical procedure. She may pass out a bruised fetus all alone.

The **failure rate for pill abortion** – those needing further surgery or other medical help – is about 1 in 10 women in Britain and China[12] while 8 in 10 in Brazil as shown here for 100 women.[13]

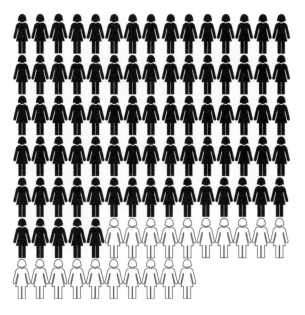

**Failure rate using the Abortion Pill in Brazil**

In the USA, Mifeprex is allowed up to 70 days after the last menstrual period. There were 22 deaths of American women associated with Mifeprex by the end of 2017.[14]

Methotrexate is used in a few US states and has produced babies born with missing toes and fingers.

The chart below (from the UK) is an approximate guide to methods commonly used.

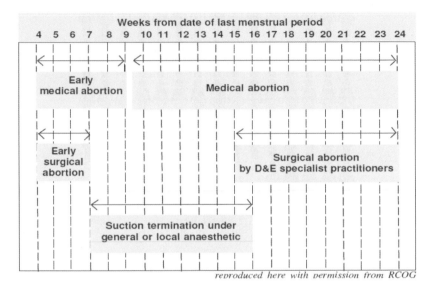

*reproduced here with permission from RCOG*

**Abortion methods by pregnancy dates**

The box below is a brief checklist of the more serious health reasons for caution before using chemical or pill abortion.

---

**Medical cautions before using the Abortion Pill**

- Allergy to any of the abortion drugs
- History of mental and emotional health problems
- Therapy with blood-thinning, anti-inflammatory or steroid drugs
- Liver or kidney disease

---

**Medical abortion after 9 weeks** is less common in the West. You may need more than one dose of Misoprostol to expel the fetus and repeated help to lessen pain.

## 5. What method and when?

Methods used at different stages of pregnancy vary from place to place. Special restrictions for the doctors and nurses may apply, not found in other procedures. So, here below is the UK's form for the two doctors to sign 'in good faith' (not the same as the patient's consent form.) Yet doctors' dishonesty has been headlines: 'We used to pre-sign forms, we used to sign forms after the operation, we used to ask the anaesthetist to do it... it was bad practice.'[15]

**EMA (early medical abortion) up to 9 weeks of pregnancy:** using EMA normally involves two visits to the hospital or clinic following initial assessment.

At the first visit, the abortion pill (Mifepristone) is to be swallowed. This blocks the hormones that help the pregnancy continue, so the pregnancy begins to be expelled. Afterwards, bleeding may continue for a couple of weeks.

At the second visit, around 1 to 3 days later, Misoprostol is given either by mouth or placed in the vagina. This causes the womb to contract and expel the pregnancy (the fetus, placenta and blood) within 4 to 6 hours. Pain, often severe, is common because the cervix is tightly shut trying to hold the fetus in and protect it.

You may go home on the same day, even if the abortion is not completed. Timing of completion cannot be predicted and may be inconvenient. Be ready to see the recognisable pregnancy parts. These, with blood, will be in your underwear for at least ten days. Stock up with plenty of sanitary pads. (See Disposal and grieving below).

# Pregnancy and Abortion

**CERTIFICATE A**

## ABORTION ACT 1967
**Not to be destroyed within three years of the date of operation**
**Certificate to be completed before an abortion is**
**performed under Section 1(1) of the Act**

I, ...........................................................................................................................................................................................................

(Name and qualifications of practitioner in block capitals)

of ...........................................................................................................................................................................................................

................................................................................................................................................................................................................

(Full address of practitioner)

**Have/have not\* seen/and examined\* the pregnant woman to whom this certificate relates at**

................................................................................................................................................................................................................

................................................................................................................................................................................................................

(full address of place at which patient was seen or examined)

on ...........................................................................................................................................................................................................

**and I** ...................................................................................................................................................................................................

(Name and qualifications of practitioner in block capitals)

of ...........................................................................................................................................................................................................

................................................................................................................................................................................................................

(Full address of practitioner)

**Have/have not\* seen/and examined\* the pregnant woman to whom this certificate relates at**

................................................................................................................................................................................................................

................................................................................................................................................................................................................

(Full address of place at which patient was seen or examined)

on ...........................................................................................................................................................................................................

**We hereby certify that we are of the opinion, formed in good faith, that in the case**

of ...........................................................................................................................................................................................................

(Full name of pregnant woman in block capitals)

of ...........................................................................................................................................................................................................

................................................................................................................................................................................................................(

Usual place of residence of pregnant woman in block capitals)

(Ring appropriate letter(s))

A   the continuance of the pregnancy would involve risk to the life of the pregnant woman greater than if the pregnancy were terminated;

B   the termination is necessary to prevent grave permanent injury to the physical or mental health of the pregnant woman;

C   the pregnancy has NOT exceeded its 24th week and that the continuance of the pregnancy would involve risk, greater than if the pregnancy were terminated, of injury to the physical or mental health of the pregnant woman;

D   the pregnancy has NOT exceeded its 24th week and that the continuance of the pregnancy would involve risk, greater than if the pregnancy were terminated, of injury to the physical or mental health of any existing child(ren) of the family of the pregnant woman;

E   there is a substantial risk that if the child were born it would suffer from such physical or mental abnormalities as to be seriously handicapped.

**This certificate of opinion is given before the commencement of the treatment for the termination of pregnancy to which it refers and relates to the circumstances of the pregnant woman's individual case.**

Signed ..............................................................................................**Date** ...........................................................................

Signed ..............................................................................................**Date** ...........................................................................

\* Delete as appropriate     DdDH005329 4/94 C8000 CC38806     Form HSA1 (revised 1991)

## 6. Abortion Pill Reversal

New methods mean women can change their mind after taking the first pill (Mifepristone) and before the second (Misoprostol). Treatment is simple, cheap and available worldwide using natural Progesterone – which is safe for both woman and fetus – to reverse the event. Seek medical advice. The success rate is about two in three cases.[16] Help and information is available through several websites.[17]

## 7. Surgical methods

'Surgical' involves an operation – hopefully under sedation or general anaesthetic, though these are not used in many parts of the world.

**Before surgery**

**Consent form:** As mentioned, for any surgery, take time and consider: Is this necessary? What are the risks?

**Premises:** Surgery should be done in an approved hospital or clinic. Beware any offer beyond approved locations where government inspectors are not seen and 'back-street' abortionists operate.

**Skills:** Check the surgeon's professional specialisation. Find one who is experienced, as this reduces complications. In the UK, clinics struggle to get these. 'Shortages of doctors trained in abortion care are so widespread,' said Prof Lesley Regan.[18] Confirming quality care – especially under pregnancy stress – is not easy. The UK Care Quality Commission may have a recent report on a clinic near you.[19]

**Anaesthetic:** This is *not* a minor procedure and there is no such thing as a minor anaesthetic. We know of sudden calamities like collapse, major drug allergies, failed anaesthesia and blood loss.

**Pre-abortion care:** In practice you should be prepared by the staff as if for full general anaesthetic, even if this is day case surgery. Things can go wrong which require skilled staff instantly.

**What you do:** After signing the consent form, you get on an operating table and put your feet up in stirrups so the surgeons can do the procedure. They drape you with sterile covers.

You should receive a local anaesthetic or a general anaesthetic where you will be unconscious. 'Local anaesthetic' can be an injection around the neck of the womb inside the vagina. Or injections in private parts are done to block pain off with variable success. Some places offer no pain relief. The fetus gets no relief from the anaesthetic.

The surgeon gains access to the womb through the vagina and cervix; they must force open the tightly shut cervix with blunt instruments called dilators. That's why the cervix can be torn – for up to 1 in a 100 women – or the womb punctured.[20] This can permanently weaken the cervix, leading to loss of the next baby.

Then they use a scraper, syringe or sucker to remove the fetus and placenta into a container. The sucker can be noisy.

After the surgery you should receive an ultrasound scan to check for remaining tissue.

**Less common abortions like late abortions (over 20 weeks)** are done by medical or surgical means. They may last about three days.[21] These procedures often mean removing the fetus in pieces – details that most people find disturbing.

Late abortion may be like an induction of labour for a wanted baby. The woman may suffer the physical pain as in birth, but the pain is felt differently without the rewards that usually follow birth.

**Stopping the heart** is often attempted before late abortion. The method is to inject potassium chloride into the heart of the fetus via a needle, technically difficult in such a small being deep in the mother's womb. The British Pregnancy Advisory Service (BPAS) say heartbeats and baby movements may continue for several hours.

BPAS (UK) quote frequent risks such as multiple needle attempts (2 women per 100), pain inserting the needle, nausea and vomiting. Less frequent are severe sepsis and death of the woman in about 1 in 1000 cases. The bowels may be injured, and open surgery of the abdomen needed to remove the fetus and repair damaged organs – including perhaps removal of the womb.[22]

**If the baby is born alive** – perhaps after failed attempts to stop the heart in the womb – mother and staff may hear crying, bringing heartrending dilemmas about next actions. There are stories available online.[23]

Many people ask, what does the baby feel? Surgeons see the fetus pulling away from a needle at 12 weeks. Pain felt in the same way as you or I know is possible from 18 weeks; these older fetuses are *super sensitive* compared to us (see also the chapter 8 'Feelings of a Fetus').

**Late surgical abortion** may be done by caesarean section (C-section) through a cut in the skin of the lower tummy – depending on several factors, including the age of the fetus. Attempts will be made by injection to make the fetus die before delivery.

**Abortion to save the mother.** Specialists can almost always save the woman's life without needing abortion.[24] The key lies in quality specialist training. In remote places, lacking specialist care, abortion to save the mother's life may be unavoidable.[25]

**Abortion for fetal disability.** Some argue it is neither needed nor helpful (see chapter 17 'Disability and Pre-birth Tests').[26]

# 8. Professionals involved

The medical world is deeply divided over abortion, so silence and secrecy are common, even at work. Doctors training in gynaecology tend to say, 'I entered medicine to save lives, not to take them.' In the USA '85% of OB/GYN's do not perform abortions.[27] UK doctors report two out of three training gynaecologists will have nothing to do with it.[28]

Among those who will perform abortions, a senior doctor said, 'I must have aborted a town the size of Barnsley.' A young doctor admitted, 'After my first abortion, I threw up in the sink. Then I got hardened.' They speak of 'feeling strange and uncomfortable' while doing it.[29]

Few medical update courses about abortion exist for British doctors, so training and professional knowledge have suffered. If that is the UK, what is the standard of care of women in poorer countries?

The Care Quality Commission quoted clinic staff in the UK, 'We have a very target-driven culture with a timed slot for each patient.' They reported, 'Registered nursing staff we spoke with felt patient care and safety were compromised by the need to "Keep on top of the list."'[30] In the USA, Catherine Anthony Adams reported, 'I spent my days urging women to terminate their pregnancies.'[31]

## 9. Disposal and grieving

Some women and couples request a burial or cremation of the remains, sometimes with a religious ceremony. You may need to insist on your wishes as reports persist in the UK of disposals in hospital incinerators.[32]

Some people have found grieving and healing helped by planting a memorial tree. In Israel, people can plant trees at Ganei Chaim for this purpose.[33]

Appendix 2 'Finding Help' offers more support.

**Grieving brothers and sisters.** The question of whether to tell siblings of the deceased is personal, but as with adults children grieve more healthily if the loss can be talked about openly.

> 'Abortion is the elephant in the room in every class I take, because it is so little talked about. Kids are curious where their sibling is,' said a teacher.[34]

## 10. After-care

Bleeding may continue from the vagina for one or two weeks, or longer. The clinic should give written information about pain management, losing further tissue and serious after-effects to report. See the 'After-effects' chapters.

GPs and clinics should arrange a physical check-up and identify severe mental illness after abortion.[35]

---

**After abortion contact a doctor if you experience...**

- Vaginal bleeding that soaks more than two sanitary pads within two consecutive hours.
- Feeling faint, sick or collapsing, as these can be signs of internal bleeding or severe infection (sepsis).
- Abdominal pain.
- Nausea, vomiting or diarrhoea for more than 24 hours.

---

**How to spot SEPSIS[36]**

If you (or anyone) has any of these seek medical help now:

- **S**lurred speech or confusion
- **E**xtreme shivering or muscle pain
- **P**assing no urine (in a day)
- **S**evere breathlessness
- **I**t feels like you're going to die
- **S**kin modelled or discoloured

Or fever above 37.5 C /99.5 F.

---

## 11. Summary

This chapter gives some insight into the procedures and facts to do with the abortion option. Your situation may demand you look at other chapters of facts also.

And finally, look back to your underlying 'problem' about this pregnancy – the one you uncovered in Part 1. People don't really *want* an abortion; it's more that they want to solve the *problem the pregnancy has highlighted*. As we saw at the start of this chapter it might be to do with your partner, your career or your finances. Once you find solutions for your problem, then a future opens up.

At that point you may feel, 'Now I don't need an abortion – I have a solution! And, I see a safe route ahead with peace of mind.'

If you still have questions keep considering the problem at hand. You can look back to the chapters on pregnancy, parenting, fostering/adoption and Appendix 2 'Finding Help' for other solutions.

---

**Charis's story**

Charis fell pregnant as a student and told her partner, 'We can't afford this and how can I study?'

John replied, 'No we can't, but even more we can't afford the emotional cost of getting rid. We will find a way.'

They found cheaper accommodation to save money. The baby care was shared with a friend. It was a hard three years but as grandparents they are happy they found help and endured those testing times.

Charis and John were speaking to the author in 2017.

---

# Chapter 12
# Abortion Law

The primary function of abortion law used to be protecting the fetus and woman from the violence of abortion, whether coerced or not. Recent relaxations of these laws weaken these protections.

Nations' laws struggle to balance the rights of a woman's choice against the rights of others; others like the fetus or the father of the fetus. And women wanting to mother may need protection from coercive pressure to abort.

**How this chapter helps you:**

1. For pregnant women and their male partners. How laws can work for your freedom and health – or against them.
2. For professionals (including counsellors). Universal responsibilities regardless of law – and where you could be sued.
3. For policy setters. Where abortion policy fails people – or does them good.

---

**True story**

The doctor confirmed my pregnancy and said, 'You don't look happy. Don't worry; have an abortion. It is safe, and your life will get back to normal.'

Molly S. White, Texas, to the authors, 2018

---

While millions have won the right to choose abortion in a safer setting than 'back-street', legalisation has exposed countless women to abortion with little information about the problems that can follow.

**This chapter covers:**

Legal protections and loopholes – often using the UK as an example.

1. The USA, Canada and Australia
2. Informed consent
3. Sex selection for a boy or a girl
4. Underage teens
5. Men and the law
6. Broken safety net – the UK law
7. Duties of a doctor
8. Rights to a second opinion
9. Conscientious objection by professionals
10. Children harmed by abortion

---

**Pregnant women and partners** remember:

Laws granting 'abortion on request' cannot guarantee low risks to the woman. As other chapters show, the range of health risks remain – even when its done by 'approved' providers rather than 'backstreet.'[1]

---

**Globally,** countless abortions happen on the supposed grounds it is safer than a birth. But, under oath in court, the public is not convinced of that. Juries in North America and Australia have weighed the evidence for birth versus abortion and convicted abortion professionals of failing to warn the woman that abortion is riskier than birth.[1,2]

Given these risks, abortion law is your vital protection. It was also *meant* to ensure a woman can give *informed* consent of her own freewill. If only this always happened in real life – which is why this chapter is vital for you.

Abortion is wholly illegal in a few states of Africa, Asia, South America and Iran.[3]

**The Republic of Ireland** brought in abortion on request up to 12 weeks gestation in 2018. And up to 24 weeks if the woman's life or health is at risk, or so called 'lethal' illnesses in the fetus are thought to be present.

Question: Irish Gynaecologists are paid more to abort than to deliver the baby. Does that help the law work impartially or not in the hands of doctors?[4]

The Irish repealed the Eight Amendment: that the life of the fetus was of equal value to the mother's. The wording of their law is now like the much-misused UK Abortion Act 1967 – see below.

**The Northern Irish** women are having liberal abortion imposed on them from Westminster (21 October 2019). The Republican parties, like Sinn Fein, of the Northern Ireland Assembly refused to convene to debate this new law – effectively allowing it in.

Hundreds of healthcare staff opposed the changes and mass protests crowded Stormont.[5]

**Coercion and forced abortion.**

Pressure into unwanted abortion can come from health professionals, partners, parents and overseers of women in the sex industry. It happens despite codes of good medical practice condemning professional coercion.

So, in many areas of the world, the woman's absolute right to say 'No' at any stage needs major review and re-enforcement.[6,7]

## 1. The USA, Canada and Australia

In 2019 amid fast moving changes, 'US states introduced new anti-abortion legislation that would ban the procedure as soon as a fetal heartbeat can be detected ... 30 states introduced some form of abortion ban,' (BBC in May 2019).[8] While other states, like New York, have legalised it up to birth.

Various US states say the doctor must inform patients about the association of abortion with breast cancer and infertility, as well as the scientific evidence of pain felt by the fetus during his or her end. (See the chapter Feelings of the Fetus)

Even if an adverse risk is described by some experts, but not generally accepted by all the medical profession, the US physician must still tell their patient of this potential risk. This is the legal doctrine of 'informed consent.'[9]

Abortion up to birth is legal in a few countries such as Canada, some US states and Victoria in Australia. Victoria allows it 'on request' up to 24 weeks of pregnancy – then tighter controls apply to birth. England, Wales and Scotland allow it to birth 'in emergency' but this is hardly ever used.[10]

## 2. Informed consent

Informed consent is meant to be about trusting your professionals to give all the information you need, demonstrating a respect for your right to decide for yourself. The 'Montgomery tightening' came about because that trust was abused in a non-abortion case.

This landmark English legal case in 2015 tightened consent rights in favour of the patient. Now, a woman must receive *written* information from the health professionals on *every possible* risk associated with the procedure.

Decision-making should be shared between the woman and the doctor.[11] Both doctor and patient are legally bound to refuse abortion unless the legal criteria are met. We gather lawyers are poised to do a test case.

Real choice or fake? Other options to abortion must be offered, otherwise she has 'no choice' and no legal consent under EU law.[12]

**What to expect** where care is high quality:

- Expect full information on the three options: parenting, adoption and abortion.[13]
- Expect written information on risks; impartial, accurate and evidence-based – for physical, emotional and fertility risks – not forgetting the risk of lethal premature birth of children born early due to prior abortion.
- Every woman should be offered a trained pregnancy counsellor at every stage.[14]
- The woman's spiritual beliefs should be explored and respected.[15]

While professionals often aim to be impartial, cases of health professionals telling women what they should do keep surfacing, for example:

---

**A 16-year-old migrant in England**

She made clear she wanted to have the baby. She was backed up by both parents, who were in the clinic and promising practical support.

Yet she was reduced to tears by the pressure of two GPs and a nurse pushing her to have an abortion 'for her good.'[16]

---

## 3. Abortion to get a boy or a girl

Abortion on the grounds of choosing the sex of the baby remains unlawful in the UK.[17] Even so British doctors are finding ways around the law.[18]

Sex selection in China, India and Georgia, for instance, has created a men over women imbalance due to millions of missing women – leaving men without hope of a wife. The UN warns of rising sexual violence and human trafficking resulting from this.[19]

## 4. Underage teens

UK law (apart from Northern Ireland) permits a young person under 16 to give her own consent for abortion without parental knowledge. But the professionals must be satisfied she can understand and retain all the possible complications and consequences – both immediate and long-term.

Many experienced carers are incredulous how this can be achieved. And hurried consultations slash holes in the legal safety net – see the chapter 'Teens – Special Care.'

Common decency suggests that parents should be involved where possible. And polling found that 86% of Britons agree that a parent or guardian's consent should be required for children under 15.[20]

## 5. Men and the law

Legally, the father of the fetus has no say in a UK abortion decision nor in many other countries. This helps explain why men are often passive in the decision-making process and walk off leaving the woman lonely and without real choice. (More in chapter 16, 'Men'.)

## 6. Broken safety net – the UK law

Back in 1967 the UK Abortion Act was passed to protect doctors and patients in difficult moral and clinical decisions for 'hard cases.' A new law was also needed due to 'back-street' abortions and growing pressure for legal abortion. Many other countries followed this lead.

The law has never functioned with integrity and many agree it's a broken safety net full of holes. It soon unleashed clear-cut abortion on request – which shows how 'hard cases make bad laws.' Risks were brushed aside and most people began believing it was safe, simple and sorts the problem. Fifty years on people are waking up to their vulnerability to so called 'legal' abortion.

Listening, for many years, to colleagues' disregard for the legal wording, 'two doctors must agree *in good faith,'* makes me question, are these the most abused words covering human destruction in British legal history?

The new Act was meant to balance the well-being of the pregnant woman, her unborn and any existing children. But doctors can hold different opinions on 'well-being.' This created the unpredictable use of the law where anything goes. Some say that was intended from the start.

The so-called 'legal' abortions of England, Scotland and Wales are almost always justified on the legal form on the grounds they should *improve* the mental health of the woman compared to letting her give birth naturally (see the legal grounds below). As we said, there has never been evidence of solid health benefits.

As a GP I commonly came across gynaecologists' letters to her GP, after the procedure, only saying, *'Unwanted pregnancy'* – without giving legal reasons for their action. Such letters could be challenged in court on threats to the patient's safety.

In the earliest days of the Abortion Act 1967, psychiatrists warned of harms to the woman from using abortion; their evidence, though debated, has only grown until now (see the Emotional and Mental risks chapter.)

Among medical colleagues in real life I noticed silence reigned over 'legality;' but the more flagrant said in effect, 'good faith means I can do what I like' – even while proceeding with abortions. (See the chapters 'Abortion Explored' and 'After-effects').[1]

**The legal grounds for English and Welsh** abortion state:

*Two doctors* must decide *'in good faith'*, that a woman meets the legal grounds for an abortion under one of the following (the form is shown on page 94):

(A) The continuance of the pregnancy would involve *risk to the life* of the pregnant woman greater than if the pregnancy were terminated.

But remember, science on millions of women shows termination is the greater *risk to the life* of the pregnant woman; it's so from 180 days afterwards and for the next 25 years (see chapters 14 and 22.)

(B) that the termination is necessary to prevent grave permanent injury to the *physical or mental* health of the pregnant woman [no time-limit, up to birth].

(C) the pregnancy has NOT exceeded its 24th week and that the continuance of the pregnancy would involve *risk, greater* than if the pregnancy were terminated, of injury to the *physical or mental* health of the pregnant woman.

(D) the pregnancy has NOT exceeded its 24th week and that the continuance of the pregnancy would involve risk, greater than if the pregnancy were terminated, of injury to the physical or mental health of *any existing child(ren)* of the family of the pregnant woman.

(E) that there is a substantial risk that if the child were born it would suffer from such physical or mental abnormalities as to be *seriously handicapped* [no time limit, so up to birth and no clarity what *seriously handicapped* means – so anything goes, such as cleft lip which is easily corrected].

Two 'medical practitioners' must sign for each abortion under one of these grounds. Yet the abortion pill is being administered by nurse practitioners alone in the UK, because of a loophole in the law. There remains a duty on professionals who are diligent to meet patients in person and examine and discuss which choice harms most.

In Britain recently, a handful at the top of the Royal College of Obstetricians and Gynaecologists are pressing to decriminalise abortion. (Remember their monopoly, only their members can provide and police the procedure.)

Yet, the public remain wisely cautious, with 72% supporting the existing abortion law that criminalises abortion beyond 24 weeks of gestation except for major abnormality or when the woman's life is in danger.[21]

Among women, 70% would like the current upper limit of 24 weeks to be lowered. 59% would like this to be 16 weeks or lower.[22]

Perhaps women know intuitively what science confirms: *tighter* legal restrictions on abortion mean *increased safety* for women (see chapter 22 'Mortality of Women').

## 7. Duties of a doctor

British doctors must understand their pregnant patient's thoughts, feelings and personal beliefs. Hence best practise makes it their duty to see patients in person.

For excellent joint decision-making between patient and doctor it demands time to chat and repeat clinic visits before a decision is made. Women and partners are advised to check online for news reports, and in the UK the CQC red flags for unsafe local clinics – perhaps where they are pre-signing batches of abortion forms without seeing the women.

## 8. Rights to a second opinion

In the UK, if the doctor believes there are no legal grounds, and it is more likely to harm the woman, or they have a conscientious objection – then the patient can seek a second opinion. The doctor must help her see another doctor, but they need not find a doctor who promises an abortion – it's their *professional judgement* about the law and her health that overrides.[23]

---

**As a woman,** before deciding:

- 'Am I confident this professional is expert to inform me about such a big decision on my health?'
- 'Has this clinic a recent an independent "excellent" quality status from the Care Quality Commission?'

You are free to walk away.

---

## 9. Conscientious objection by professionals

**In the UK,** around 2 in 3 medical staff refuse to take a part in abortions, arguing, 'I trained to save lives and doing abortions feels odd' or 'repugnant'. [24,25]

**In the USA,** healthcare professionals have a right not to perform or assist in abortions.[26]

**Canadian doctors** in all provinces have rights under conscience. The CMA (Canadian Medical Association) exempts them from providing or referring patients for abortion, but there should be no delay in provision. They should inform the patient of their moral and clinical opinion so another opinion can be sought if wanted.[27]

## 10. Children harmed by abortion

Freeing up abortion law has not protected unborn humans – including abortion causing the next child born to arrive dangerously premature. As adults these people could sue the gynaecologist for causing their preterm birth, cerebral palsy and a lifetime of pain and disability.[28]

**Policymakers and the public** ponder this: Doctors designed much of the abortion law. Doctors make the legal judgements on the day. Doctors oversee or do the procedure. Doctors are paid for it. Doctors police it. Doctors record and store the evidence out of reach.

Does this inspire good care or corrupt practise?

**In summary,** it is wise to *know for yourself* the legal information that can protect free informed consent, life and health. 'Forewarned is forearmed' because you too may come under pressure from partners or professionals that is hard to refuse.

# Chapter 13
# Early After-effects

This and the next chapter summarise the unintended side-effects during and after abortion. 'Early' means during the procedure and soon after. The next chapter covers later effects, like premature birth (which impacts the children's well-being and lives), infertility, women's deaths, emotional troubles and breast cancer.

Side-effects can be a sensitive, even secretive subject, but they are important for reaching an informed choice due to their potential to impact health and happiness.

The risks outlined here are *possible* after-effects. No one can predict what happens to *you*; but some issues are more likely than others. It depends on your age, type of abortion, previous pregnancies and any STIs (sexually transmitted infections) in your history.

Science cannot say that abortion *causes all* these complications, but it can for some of them. It is quite a daunting list of issues (Part 3 of the guide goes deeper).

These are not 'back-street' abortion problems, they can happen in the best care. They are public knowledge from peer-reviewed studies, often based on huge populations in North America, Britain and Scandinavia. Fresh Indian, South American, African and Chinese research is finding still more.

**Miscarriage** (spontaneous abortion) shares some side-effects with abortion, but they are milder. A miscarriage is more likely to happen when conceived in the first 3 months after an abortion.

**Medical (Pill) abortion** tends to bring more early problems than surgical methods (see chapter 11 'Abortion Explored'). Further surgery is just one of these; both medical and surgical methods had similar risks of further surgery according to the British RCOG.[1]

**This chapter covers:**

1. Pain
2. Infection
3. Vaginal bleeding
4. Emotional distress
5. Incomplete or failed abortion
6. Damage to the womb
7. Born alive
8. Summary

---

**Annie's story (part 1)**

Annie has just turned 26 when she gets pregnant by James. She has a legal abortion and goes back to work.

Sadly, this is followed by an infection, which she does not notice at the time. The germs silently block up her Fallopian tubes. Unknown to Annie, her eggs can no longer travel to her womb; meanwhile her life carries on as if all is well, with regular menstrual periods.

(Part 2 of Annie's story is on page 120)

---

All medical procedures carry a risk, but evidence suggests that several side-effects of abortion are associated with a higher risk than a full-term pregnancy and birth. In fact, birth gives the woman a lower risk of death (due to various causes) in the following years than not being pregnant or after an abortion.

## 1. Pain

Pain is a natural signal that something needs attention. No one can say the level of pain you will feel during and after abortion, but there will be some.

The reason is that both medical and surgical abortion involve stretching open the tightly closed neck of the womb, which is naturally contracting to keep the fetus inside.

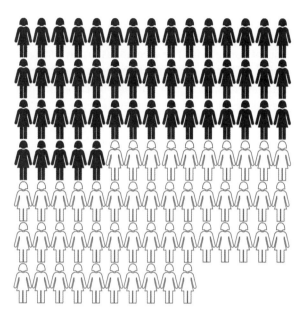

**50 out of 100 American women using medical abortion rated their abdominal pain 'severe'.[2]**

25 out of 100 British women reported pain levels of 7/10 (where 10 is the greatest imaginable).[3]

**Pain soon after abortion – when to be concerned**

Persistent or severe pain signal a serious side-effect, like internal bleeding or a punctured organ. Don't stay alone or at home – see your doctor the same day.

**Factors affecting the level of pain**

Women can suffer increased pain at abortion if they are anxious, or if it has been a long procedure. The atmosphere in the clinic can worsen pain.[4]

Research shows pain after abortion is more likely for younger females, when it is a woman's first pregnancy and those of white race.

Women under sedation seem to suffer more from stress disorder, depression and physical ill-health one month and three months afterwards than those having a general anaesthetic (fully unconscious).[5]

## 2. Infection

This is a significant concern for the woman, as Annie discovered, because it can do a variety of harms. The infection can spread from the womb to the Fallopian tubes, making her infertile by blocking the passage of the egg as this picture shows.

### FALLOPIAN TUBE OBSTRUCTION

British gynaecologists say 10 in 100 women are infected from the abortion procedure and it can be associated with complications – vaginal discharge, painful sex and pelvic inflammatory disease (PID).[6] Antibiotics given before an abortion don't always work. Follow-on pregnancies can miscarry or be premature with risk to the child of cerebral palsy or death.

---

**How to spot SEPSIS in adults[7]**

If you see the following – get urgent medical help:

**SEPSIS**

- **S**lurred speech or confusion
- **E**xtreme shivering or muscle pain
- **S**evere breathlessness
- **I**t feels like you're going to die
- **S**kin modelled or discoloured

Also a fever above 37.5 C /99.5 F. or unpleasant vaginal discharge.

---

Even with the best care infection can get a grip fast, which is why Jeremy Hunt, then Secretary of State for Health, said to Great Britain in 2017:

---

'Every death from sepsis [life-threatening infection] is a tragedy, yet too often the warning signs are missed.'

---

## 3. Vaginal bleeding

This can be expected for up to ten days, and the blood loss may be a lot. Parts of the fetus may be mixed with the blood. Further surgery can be needed to stop the bleeding and sometimes blood transfusions.

---

**Bleeding from the vagina**

*– call for medical help on the same day*

if you are using more than two sanitary pads in two hours in a row.

**Excessive vaginal bleeding**

*– call for medical help right now*

if you see lots of blood, feel faint, collapse or have severe pain.

---

## 4. Emotional distress

At first, women can feel relief that the pregnancy is over. Others, however, experience a devastating dive in their mood and are upset with the people around them, including the abortion staff. Then, seeing the remains of the fetus, perhaps alone at home, can arouse feelings of loss and regret. Sharing these feelings can be difficult because you hoped to feel better, not worse.

Mental breakdown or psychosis can happen soon after, so women should be reviewed after each abortion, though this often fails to happen in the UK.

If you have had any previous pregnancy loss such as a miscarriage, an abortion or a stillbirth, these are risk factors which may need more counselling. Adding a new loss, through abortion, may make matters worse. Gently give yourself, or others you are walking alongside, permission to discuss sensitive feelings around past loss.

**Personal checklist of your mental risk** (from the American Psychological Association)[8]

If you are considering abortion be more cautious if any of these apply:

- Your pregnancy is wanted or meaningful.[9]
- You are facing pressure from others to abort.
- There is opposition by partners, family or friends.
- You are unsure about the decision.
- There is lack of social support from others.
- You have certain personality traits, such as low self-esteem, a pessimistic outlook or feel you have no control over life.
- You have a history of mental health problems.
- You have feelings of shame.
- You feel the need for secrecy.
- You are prone to use of avoidance and denial coping strategies.
- You have feelings of commitment to the pregnancy.
- You are not sure that you can cope with the abortion.
- You have had a previous abortion(s).
- You have had a previous abortion late in pregnancy.

More at Appendix 1 'ABC of Spiritual Beliefs' and Appendix 2 'Finding Help'.

## 5. Incomplete or failed abortion

This means failure for all the fetal parts and placenta to be removed, or the fetus is still living. This happens in around 4 to 8 women per 100 for surgical and medical methods respectively.[10] Further D&C surgery is required.

## 6. Damage to the womb

Tearing of the cervix (neck of the womb) by surgical instruments is associated with premature birth of the next pregnancy. Estimates of damage range from between 1 to 15 women in a 100.[11]

The surgeon can accidentally hole the womb, affecting up to 4 women in 1,000 abortions. Punctures can lead to infection and peritonitis. Peritonitis can glue the pelvic organs together as 'adhesions'. Adhesions can cause painful sex, fertility issues and other effects long after.

But US researchers found womb puncture *actually* occurred 7 times more often than the surgeons thought.[12] The risk of puncture is lower when the surgeon is experienced but finding experienced abortion surgeons in the UK is hard.[13]

## 7. Born alive

The fetus or their twin may survive. Sarah Smith can be heard talking about her experience on The Abortion Survivors website.[14]

In 2008, 66 British babies were born alive this way and year by year some grow up and speak of how they feel about their parents and society.[15]

## 8. Summary

Love yourself, don't bury bad feelings, and get help early for low mood or suicidal thoughts. Share your worry or pain with someone you trust.

If you had an abortion, you may be suffering some after-effects and feel down. No problem is beyond help or hope (see Appendix 2 'Finding Help').

Think carefully before consenting. If you feel pressured to abort, look for somewhere safe to go. There you can make your own decision in your own time.

Now take a read of the longer term in chapter 14 'Later After-effects'.

# Chapter 14
# Later After-effects

While some people seem to go through abortion without problems, it helps to know – both before and after abortion – that hidden risks can appear in the following months or much later.

Later after-effects associated with abortion often overlap with the ones we looked at in the previous chapter. To read them again, flip back to page 109 now.

Some people brush aside the long-term issues; but its the pregnant woman who must live with the consequences to her life and health.

---

**There was a woman called Ivy**

Complications can last into old age – 84-year-old Ivy comes to mind. She is still grieving her lost baby. Her first partner left her. Maybe his grief contributed to their relationship breakdown (for information on relationships, see chapter 16 'Men'). Later, she got pregnant again and had a child born premature. Sadly, cerebral palsy made the care for that child very demanding.

---

**This chapter covers:**

1. Pain and pelvic inflammatory disease (PID)
2. Emotional and mental after-effects
3. Preterm birth and future children
4. Infertility, ectopic pregnancy and placenta praevia
5. Breast cancer after abortion
6. Mortality of women

## 1.  Pain and pelvic inflammatory disease (PID)

Living with daily pain deeply disrupts normal life and sleep. Depressive mood and suicidal ideas can be just around the corner.

As we saw, any infection soon after abortion can turn into painful PID. This chronic condition usually starts with vaginal discharge, pelvic pain and discomfort, sometimes felt as deep internal pain during sex. PID is associated with sub-fertility.[1]

This graphic shows that among 100 women with Chlamydia, the commonest link for going on to PID was those who had had a legal abortion.[2]

**In 100 women with Chlamydia using legal abortion –**
**from 27% (black) to 72% (black + grey) may get PID. (9 studies)**

Chlamydia screening should be done before any abortion and treated with antibiotics. However, this does not guarantee against PID afterwards.[3]

**Damage to the lining of the womb** (Asherman's syndrome)

This results from scar tissues following surgery (D&C) for medical or surgical abortion. It can show up as abnormal menstruation, recurrent miscarriage and infertility. It is increasing worldwide and linked with surgical abortion and surgery done to complete failed medical (pill) abortion.[4]

Chinese studies found 4 in 10 women (42.4%) with Asherman's syndrome and infertility were post-abortion.[5]

## 2. Emotional and mental after-effects

Any unplanned pregnancy stirs up many emotions and they vary in character. Then the pregnant woman needs all the emotional support she can get (see Appendix 2 'Finding Help').

If she already has a mental health condition like depression, or had it in the past, abortion likely worsens the condition and is grounds not to abort. Previous puerperal psychosis (a major mental illness in pregnancy) is a strong reason not to abort.[6]

Prof. David Fergusson (who was pro-abortion) found there were moderate increases in risks of mental diseases like depression after abortion, even in those with no previous history of mental illness.[7] He urged the New Zealand government to make this warning government policy. In addition, abortion brought no benefits to the mental health of women with unwanted pregnancies.[8]

'The mental health benefits of childbirth and children outweigh the mental health harms of abortion.'[9]

We met Annie in the previous chapter, see part 1 of her story on page 112.

**Annie's story (part 2)**

Annie does not realise she got an infection during her abortion at 26 ...

Two years later, Annie meets Alan when she is 28 and they want children. Alan's sperm cannot get past the blockage in her tubes due to infection acquired at her previous abortion and natural pregnancy is impossible.

This delays Annie's first full-term pregnancy (FFTP). After a year of trying for a baby, she has infertility tests and they go for fertility treatment by in vitro fertilisation (IVF).

Three cycles of IVF stress Annie's relationship with Alan and they drift apart. She is pregnant from the third treatment cycle and, although now alone, she wants to be a parent.

Baby Islay is born extremely premature at 24 weeks gestation – so early that it could be linked to the abortion Annie had at 26. Islay suffers a brain bleed when she is 10 days old due to her preterm birth. The bleed leaves her with cerebral palsy and a floppy arm and leg for life.

Now a single mum, Annie struggles with work, alongside caring for Islay, and her income drops. Her housing condition worsens. She thinks of working in the sex industry.

Annie's story may sound extreme, but it is not exceptional to meet people like her while working in healthcare.

Annie's singleness affected her childcare and her income, so she had to live in a bedsit and started to drink too much. She found a post-abortion organisation who helped her out of poverty and became a great mother.

Compared to women giving birth, those having abortion were more likely to abuse substances during their next pregnancy: 10 times more marijuana use, 5 times more other illicit drugs and twice as likely alcohol – with known risks to the baby.[10] Annie's story reminds the strong to offer support to the vulnerable.

- **Suicide and self-harm.** These become more likely soon after abortion, and the father of the fetus is at higher risk of suicide as well.[11]
- **Regret and long-term guilt.** These can be experienced by both women and men, sometimes into old age. They can be the root of physical illness, violence and depression. It can be difficult to come to terms with such feelings, but in the right hands, help can be effective.

Margaret and Iris were both elderly women who approached us asking if they could ever be forgiven for previous abortions. Since they were both Christians, they were directed to a pastor gaining heart-warming benefits (see Appendix 1 'ABC of Spiritual Beliefs').

Untreated guilt among other feelings can become a toxic mixture. Could it be connected to intimate partner violence linked with a past abortion? All this adds up to higher rates of suicide, accidents and murder. (See chapter 22 'Mortality'.)

- **Domestic Violence (Intimate Partner Violence) and murder.** A World Health Organisation study in 2005 showed that domestic violence is related to an increase in teenage pregnancy and induced abortion – often used under threat.

In 1997, Finnish research found that after an abortion the woman was over four times more likely to be murdered. Whereas after a birth, she was a third *less* likely to be killed among 281 women who died up to one year after the end of pregnancy.[12]

Overall, 1 in 10 mental health problems in our communities are associated with prior abortion.[13]

## 3. Preterm birth and future children

Why this rather dramatic title? Because there is a higher risk to follow-on children of being born prematurely after an abortion. Babies born too early are at greater risk of cerebral palsy, infection and death.

A study, combining 37 studies, found that one previous abortion made a preterm birth in the follow-on pregnancy 27% more likely. In the UK, this would raise a woman's risk of giving birth prematurely from 7% to about 10% (in other words, 1 in 10 births).

Two or more previous abortions made preterm birth 62% more likely (see chapter 20 'Premature Birth After Abortion').

---

**Sadly, as we go to press...**

The weakest citizens are most under threat.

The biggest ever study of evidence will soon show a *5 times* increased risk of *very preterm birth* after 3 or more abortions – the very ones at most risk of dying or permanent brain damage.

(See chapter 20 'Premature Birth After Abortion'.)

---

**Cerebral palsy (CP)** in babies is a risk of premature birth. Unfortunately for children born early, at 28 weeks or less, the relative risk of CP may be 60 times higher.[14]

**Damage to the cervix** (neck of the womb) can bring about premature birth. Forced widening of the cervical passage at abortion can damage its ability to hold a pregnancy in. The Royal College of Obstetricians and Gynaecologists puts the risk of damage at up to 1 in 100 surgical abortions.[15]

Other threats to your next children are as follows:

**Miscarriages.** Cervix damage may contribute to early miscarriages if another pregnancy occurs within three months of an abortion. So, it is better to delay conception at least three months after an abortion.[16] A Chinese study showed the risk of miscarriage was about 2.5 times higher in women who had had two or more abortions, than women with no previous abortion.[17]

**Stillbirth of subsequent babies.** Stillbirth means a baby who dies before birth. The risk increases by nearly five times after abortion if infection gets in (1 in 10 have infection).[18] The link between may lie in a previous abortion causing an infection, which lurks hidden till it harms the next pregnancy.

## 4. Infertility, ectopic pregnancy and placenta praevia

Here are several more reasons why a woman's ability to conceive and deliver a healthy baby may be blocked by previous abortion.

- **Inability to conceive again.** As we saw, abortion often brings infection into the reproductive organs (1 in 10 abortions[19]) which makes tube blockage more likely. A tubal block means another pregnancy is impossible without surgery or the challenging road of in-vitro fertilisation (IVF). One study shows the risk rising about 7 times after abortion.[20] (See chapter 19 'Infertility After Abortion'.)
- **Ectopic pregnancies.** Ectopic pregnancy has been linked to previous abortion. An Australian study found that a woman's risk of ectopic was 7–10 times higher with Pelvic Inflammatory Disease (PID), which is itself linked to abortion.[21] One in 10 women with PID will have an ectopic.[22]

## Normal pregnancy      Ectopic pregnancy

**Normal pregnancy grows in the womb but ectopic grows in the tube.[23]**

- **The risk of placenta praevia.** When the placenta lies too low in the womb; it is prone to bleed through the cervix with risk to the mother and baby. The risk rises after induced abortions.[24]

- **Fertility falls in women over 30.** Delay in first full-term delivery leaves you older to start a family.

## 5. Breast cancer after abortion

The lifetime risk of developing breast cancer has risen from 1 in 8 to 1 in 6 women in the UK.[25] There are several reasons why. The rise in abortion use, hormonal contraceptives and HRT can be tracked against this increased risk.

In the USA, abortion was legalised in 1973 and the breast cancer incidence has risen since 1975. The cumulative lifetime risk has risen from 1 in 12 to 1 in 8 women since 1975.[26]

Across Ireland, women enjoy a lower risk, which can be tracked against their lower numbers of abortion and less use of hormonal contraception – although now, both abortion legalisation and higher hormonal contraceptive use may provoke a rise in breast cancer soon.

**The critical factor:** age at first full-term pregnancy (FFTP). Take a young woman who is in her first pregnancy. What is her risk of breast cancer?

---

**Rachel – what's her risk of breast cancer?**

Rachel is 18 and in her first pregnancy.

She chooses to have an abortion, which delays her first full-term pregnancy (FFTP) for five years. At 23 she gets married, becomes pregnant and gives birth to Alfie. She helps lower her breast cancer risk slightly by deciding to breastfeed him.

Rachel studies the evidence, so she realises that delaying her FFTP by five years made her lifetime risk for breast cancer rise by one fifth.

She is glad she avoided another five-year delay in FFTP till she was 28. If she had waited till 28, then her lifetime cancer risk would rise another fifth, that's 40% higher. [27]

---

This protective effect of full-term pregnancy on breast cancer risk has been known since the Middle Ages and the way nuns got more breast cancer.

However, women in their early 20s who start having children experience no permanent rise in breast cancer risk – in fact a lowered risk over their lifetimes.

---

**Annie's story (part 3)**

Fast forward 30 years, and Annie (from earlier in this chapter) is 60. Her periods have stopped. While showering one day, she finds a lump in her breast and thinks, 'I must go and see my doctor today.'

Five years after the breast cancer was found and removed, she is grateful to be one who has survived the cancer diagnosis for five years. She attends counselling because she is trying to break free from the cycle of regret over the abortion in her 20s.

---

*All women are advised to carry out regular self-checks for breast cancer.*

See how here www.nationalbreastcancer.org/breast-self-exam

## 6. Mortality of women

Hidden deaths from abortion have come to light through studying all females of Finland and Denmark. Having lifestyles like the UK and USA we can learn from them.

Thankfully, deaths *during* the procedure are rare, but do happen with both surgical and medical methods. Infection is the culprit in a third of these tragedies.[28]

The delayed deaths come from suicides, intimate partner violence, accidents and strokes. They begin 6 months after abortion through to 25 years later.

The higher risk of death is up to 6 times higher than following childbirth and 4 times higher than not being pregnant.[29] So, pregnancy with birth is safest!

---

**How can we imagine a woman's abortion risk?**

Compare risks with everyday events like road use during one year.[30] It gives *an idea* of risks although we are not comparing the same.

A woman's risk of death in the year after an abortion is up to 20 times higher than her risk of dying in a year of road use.

---

**Repeat abortions multiply women's deaths?**

The next 2 charts show at a glance the effect on women's risk after abortion compared to giving birth. The figures come from 1 million Danish women following their abortion. The numbers lost accumulate because the raised risk persists for 25 years.[31]

**Chart 1**

**Women's chances of dying are higher following abortions – research on one million Danish women**

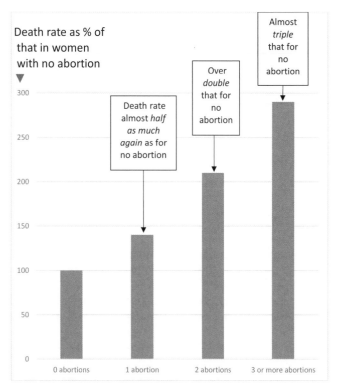

**Women's long-term death rate as % of that in women who have had no abortions, for women with various numbers of abortions**
(adjusted for year of woman's birth, age at last pregnancy, number of natural losses and number of births.)
From table 3 of Coleman PK, Reardon DC, Calhoun BC. Reproductive history patterns and long-term mortality rates: a Danish, population-based record linkage study. *Eur J Public Health*. 2013;23(4):569-574. doi:10.1093/eurpub/cks107.

On the other hand, several births lengthen the lives of mothers compared to the non-pregnant women, as Chart 2 shows.

## Chart 2

## Births confer longer life expectancy

### Women's mortality falls after giving birth at least twice – research on one million Danish women

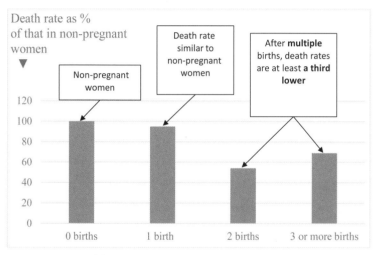

**Women's long-term death rate as % of that in women who are not pregnant ('0 births'), for women with different numbers of births**

(adjusted for year of woman's birth, age at last pregnancy, number of induced abortions and number of natural losses)

From table 3 of Coleman PK, Reardon DC, Calhoun BC. Reproductive history patterns and long-term mortality rates: a Danish, population-based record linkage study. *Eur J Public Health*. 2013;23(4):569-574. doi:10.1093/eurpub/cks107.

As a woman, if you feel vulnerable, support and help is essential. In London in 2014 there were 6 times higher rates of Inter Partner Violence (IPV) among women having abortion than women receiving antenatal care to give birth. The Royal College of Obstetricians and Gynaecologists recommends doctors to use child and women protection services after identifying women at risk of IPV around pregnancy and especially abortion.[32]

More on mortality in chapter 22.

# Chapter 15
# Teens – Special Care

Are you a teenager and think you may be pregnant, or your girlfriend could be? You may feel scared, especially about what your parents or teachers will say. (To check a pregnancy test, go to chapter 1 'Am I Pregnant?'.)

If pregnancy is confirmed, you may feel shocked and numb. All kinds of thoughts and feelings will fly through your head. The important thing is to keep calm because, there *is* a way forward. As a teen you are still growing, so here is information that mainly helps teens.

Teenagers often make wonderful parents and have done for centuries. But emotional and bodily differences from adults need handling with extra care.

**This chapter covers:**

1. Teens are different
2. Which way forward?
3. Thinking of abortion?
4. Parents
5. Young men
6. Emotional ill-health and suicide
7. Rape and abuse
8. Physical after-effects
9. Summary

## 1. Teens are different

Bodies are different in teenage years. The vagina and womb are still growing and more easily damaged by surgical instruments and the drugs used in abortion. A teenager is more vulnerable to bleeding and pain during and after abortion.[1]

You might find it helpful to get one or both of your parents, or a friend, to read this so that you can talk together. It helps to talk it all over with someone you trust so you come to a better understanding of what's best for you.

You probably had no plans to have a baby now! So you may feel hopeless and life is wrecked. But wait a moment – life, education, work and friends will go on! First we need to think carefully about the best way forward – and *there are ways* – trust us, as experts and friends, and together we will find the best for you.

## 2. Which way forward?

So, take plenty of time to think carefully about *all* options ahead of you. There are options (see Part 1) even if people are pushing you to abortion. Rushing into abortion means missing the rewards of thinking it over first.

Help is out there and it is worth digging for the help and alternatives there are.

Temporary fostering or adoption of the baby are time-tested ways forward. And while many families may be shocked at first we have often seen them rally round saying, 'We will help you look after this baby.' However, if this is not the case, don't do anything drastic as there are other ways forward. See Appendix 2 'Finding Help'.

---

### Isabella's story

'I found out I was pregnant in September, when I'd just turned 14, just before the school term started. I did the test in my bedroom while all my family were out. I just came downstairs and acted like I was fine.

'I went to school the next day and it really hit me then. I got really upset... the thought of it... I think I was quite numb for a while... it was very scary. I told my boyfriend, and that was all... for about two weeks.

'We went to the health clinic and they were arranging an abortion straight away for me. They did not talk through any options, but just gave me a leaflet and a follow-up appointment. My boyfriend was more scared than me, as his parents were stricter. I said I could not do it – have an abortion – and he supported me.

'As a teenage mum living at home, it's been hard to watch friends doing teen stuff and I feel I've missed out on those years. But I'm glad I kept my boy and now I know it's been the right thing.'

---

## 3. Thinking of abortion?

For your safety, it is best to let your parents know or someone you trust. Then they can help look after you and be ready if anything goes wrong. They can help with low feelings, heavy bleeding or sepsis (dangerous infection) which needs treating quickly.

They can also let the clinic know about any medical history for your safer care. The doctors may not have access to all your medical records.

> Do you remember 18-year-old Laila's story in chapter 11 'Abortion Explored'? (p83) Laila alerted us to potential problems for teens.

Abortion in teens is linked with greater risks of physical and emotional problems than in adults.[2] So, handling this decision needs great caution and lengthy exploration for the best long-term decision.

## 4. Parents

If you find your daughter is pregnant, keep calm! Nothing on earth can replace a parent or friend's non-judgemental love and acceptance as your teenager works through the initial shock.

Most parents have dreams for their children that they grow up into happy, confident adults. Reading this chapter with your teenager can help you stay supportive through a decision, aiming for their best.

Have a look at earlier chapters of this guide and talk it over. If you are a single parent, talk with a close friend or family member.[3]

Involve your daughter and the baby's father as soon as possible (in the UK, the father has legal obligations until their child is 18). Winning the teen's trust and respect without pressure, storms or threats is an investment for life – theirs and yours.

In our view, professionals who fail to involve the parents before abortion put their patient at higher risk of immediate and long-term ill health: to cope with the amount of information given (maybe over several occasions) it is doubtful to many experts whether a teenager can grasp the lifelong implications on her own.

The law for under 16s in England comes down to whether she can understand the implications for the short and long term; that's in the opinion of professionals, *not her parents*. There is no legal obligation to inform parents if her understanding is supposedly there. Naturally, this puts her at risk of secret abortion, perhaps to hide sexual abuse. Poor clinical care and poor explanation by professionals, who may have financial interests, are further risks.

At present Irish doctors get paid considerably more for doing an abortion than for a delivery. New Zealand permits abortion for girls under 16 without parental consent.

---

**My teenage birth – the gains and losses**

'I had my son when I was 15, before I had even sat my GCSEs. The positives of having a child so early in my life are that he has kept me busy and given me the incentive to do better and get a good job. Being younger, I have had more energy to give and we shall be closer in age as we grow up.

'The negative aspects are a lack of savings and difficulty in being able to afford things, along with the isolation from peers and loss of freedom which most teenagers enjoy.'[4]

---

## 5. Young men

Teenage boys may be just as surprised and scared by a pregnancy as the girl they have been sleeping with. How they deal with it depends on their character and the support from their social network including their parents. If you are one of those, let's reassure you – most parents and friends calm down and help quickly.

Some boys/men are just as affected – or worse – by abortion as some women. Numerous studies support this.[5] Parents and professionals should try to involve the father in decision-making. (More in chapter 16 'Men'.)

## 6. Emotional ill-health and suicide

This section is to take care and not to scare. Keep remembering there is hope and practical help online, by phone and locally.

Psychologist Patricia Coleman studied teenage girls' emotions. A pregnancy is seen as 'happened to' them rather than being the outcome of their own choices. So, a teenager is more inclined to opt suddenly for an abortion before looking at the problem underneath such as fear of the parents.[6]

In fact evidence suggests that having an abortion may worsen her mental state, while giving birth makes teens relieved, positive and less depressed.

Professor David Fergusson looked up the life outcomes for teenage mothers until they were 25 years old. He concluded, 'Abortion in young women may be associated with increased risk of mental health problems.'[7]

A US study in 2006 showed that adolescent girls who abort 'unwanted' pregnancies are five times more likely to seek help later for psychological and emotional problems than their peers who continue to give birth.[8] Paranoia, drug misuse and psychosis are commoner later.[9] In high school students, suicide attempts were between six and ten times more likely after abortion.[10]

The next two charts from a British study compare how suicidal young women felt before and after an abortion to after giving birth.[11] The height of a bar gives the number of women attempting suicide out of 1,000. Look for the age group that interests you.

Suicide Attempts
per 1,000 Women

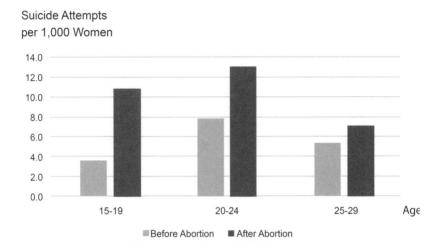

Before Abortion ■ After Abortion

**Women's suicide attempts before and after abortion, by age group**

How does abortion (above) compare with suicide attempts in women giving birth (below)?

Suicide Attempts
per 1,000 Women

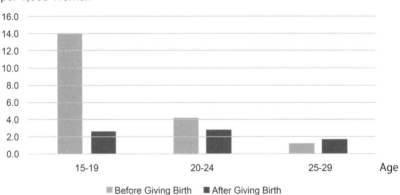

Before Giving Birth ■ After Giving Birth

**Women's suicide attempts before and after birth, by age group**

## 7. Rape and abuse

In these tragic situations, many people feel it is natural to do abortion 'to remove the problem'. But this is not so clear when we take care to discover what will *really help* the victim. Sadly, the abuse cannot be undone, and the vulnerability of teens to abortion's after-effects remain for the long-term.

We must search for paths of care and healing that support the victim long-term and go to the roots of their distress. We do not want to cause more situations like the raped American woman who told her gynaecologist, 'The abortion was like being raped again.'[12]

Even the decision-making about the fate of the child can be severely traumatising for a woman.[13]

With expert help and support, recovery is possible, as many women made mothers by rape will testify.

More help is in Appendix 1 'ABC of Spiritual Beliefs' and Appendix 2 'Finding Help'.

## 8. Physical after-effects

Infection (1 in 10 after an abortion) is a major risk for a teen. And when Chlamydia infection (an STI) is present in girls aged 13–19, then a womb infection after abortion happens in over a quarter of them, compared to a fifth of women in their twenties. Chlamydia is linked to later PID (pelvic inflammatory disease) pain, infertility and ectopic pregnancy, and the death rates for ectopic pregnancy are higher in women aged 15–19 than in older women.[14]

All the risks are higher in teens, risks like haemorrhage and others that you can find in the Early and Later After-effects chapters.

Breast cancer risks in later life rise to nine times higher in women who had an abortion before they were 18, compared to their life-long risk of breast cancer if they didn't have an abortion.

## 9. Summary

Teenagers can make good parents. We explored how they are especially vulnerable in their bodies, thinking and feeling. Hence, it is vital that the pregnant teenager and her partner are accepted, supported and well informed.

Abortion cannot get rid of the issues around the unwanted pregnancy. Other solutions to the problems of shame, secrecy and education can be found.

Help is available for teens and their families – Appendix 2 'Finding Help'.

# Chapter 16
# Men

'Men? What has abortion got to do with men? It's a women's issue, isn't it?' said a man.[1]

We explore how men feel about pregnancy and abortion. Then, we look at how relationships work through the stress of an unplanned pregnancy, dilemma and loss.

**This chapter covers:**

1. Do men matter?
2. What men feel about pregnancy
3. Men's feelings about abortion
4. Men at clinics
5. To save a relationship
6. Law and men
7. Conflict between men and women
8. Help and hope for men

Jonathan Jeffes, founder of the Restore and Rebuild post-abortion course, has been counselling women and men about abortion for over 20 years. 'Generally, the experience of the women on our courses shows that a woman will nearly always go to the man involved, tell him she is pregnant and ask him what he thinks they should do as a couple. The reply is often: "I will do whatever *you* want to do."'[2]

## 1. Do men matter?

Jeffes writes, 'The journey to an abortion clinic does not just begin with a pregnancy. It starts with a man and woman sleeping together, and it is here that men must also accept responsibility: for their behaviour towards women, in their values, in contraception and their understanding of abortion.'

'These are not just "women's issues", they are men's issues too, and whatever the story, men should be encouraged to face up to their part in an abortion decision.'

Does this help us see why abortion can be explosive between couples? Does it help us see why Father's Day may be difficult for men after abortion?

> 'There is a myth in society that says men don't care, or that men are untouched by the experience. My experience of listening to men's stories over the years is that men are deeply touched by abortion loss but struggle to talk about it.'
>
> A post-abortion counsellor

In 2015, *Long Lost Family* (on ITV) showed a meeting at St Pancras Railway Station in London. They brought together a French father and an English mother. The couple had last met one long hot summer, years before in France. The climax came when she gently confronted him, across the coffee table, regarding the abortion of their fetus that he had insisted on all those years ago. The confident, handsome man looked away. He looked at the floor; he struggled to speak.

*The Times* of London reported on the new science of why dads matter: 'Fathers' testosterone levels drop by up to 30% during their partner's pregnancies as they prepare to become caregivers; fathers are more important than the mothers in children's language development...'[3]

So how do we understand the anger that erupts between men and women over the pregnancy decision? Jeffes asks men and women on his courses, 'What is the difference between men and women?' Long discussions follow, but there is only one statement with which nearly everyone can agree:

> 'Both men and women tell us that in a crisis a woman will look to a man for protection, and a man will instinctively want to protect her.'

This raises gender issues. But, less encouragingly, he continues, 'Perhaps men also have an instinct to protect themselves from sacrificial responsibility. So, although initially a woman can think "Do whatever you want" is supportive, later she may come to see this as a conscious withdrawing of the man's natural protection – in fact a betrayal.

'She may also feel he is not protecting the child, as she instinctively wants him to, even if she eventually chooses an abortion. This sense of betrayal is a powerful source of the anger that a woman can feel after an abortion.'

Unfortunately, it is often the case in trying to help pregnant women that the responsible male is nowhere to be seen. When able to talk to the partner and explore their feelings, almost all were aware of responsibility towards the woman and the fetus they had conceived.

## 2. What men feel about pregnancy

Monica Heisy, in the British youth magazine *Vice*, said, 'In the few studies regarding the male reaction to the news of a pregnancy, their responses mirrored one of the most common responses of newly pregnant women: *ambivalence*' (meaning unsure of what to think and do now).

'Upon the discovery of a *hoped-for* pregnancy there is pride combined with fear, happiness combined with dread – both men and women tend to feel a mixture of angst and excitement.'

And, when 'confronted with an *unwanted* pregnancy these feelings, according to a Swedish study, are almost the same for both men and women... more than half expressed ambivalent feelings about the coming abortion, using words like anxiety, responsibility, guilt, relief and grief.'[4]

## 3. Men's feelings about abortion

Monica Heisy tells of Paul, aged 28, who was at drama school when his girlfriend, a classmate, got pregnant...

'The experience was a bit like being painted out, unintentionally,' Paul told her.

Monica spoke to six men and discovered they all had a similar story to Paul's. They can often feel excluded from decisions regarding the pregnancy they have helped create.

A man known to the authors took his life within a day of the abortion of the baby he had fathered. He had been pleading with his partner to let him look after the child and promised a good home for them all. His last note said life was not worth living without his child.[5]

Another dynamic is at work as well. Brad Mattes of the Men and Abortion websites says,

'Conscience is what hurts when everything else feels so good.'[6]

Mattes continues, 'The way men process hurt is through physical and emotional reactions. Anger to abortion loss is the most common reason men explode. But this may happen at times when others are nearby, or even the man himself doesn't know why he's exploding.'

'Other symptoms of grief and guilt are depression, anxiety and abuse of drugs and alcohol. These make it difficult to decide anything or hold down a job.'

'It feels like a deep dark secret that taints life, but stays hidden socially then reappears, perhaps as a workaholic lifestyle. He feels like a fugitive from something that is just too hard to face, so he might become a devil-may-care risk taker on his motorbike.'

'Men and women's reasons for *wanting to end a pregnancy* were also the same and include wanting children later, wanting to be able to provide for their family at a level they felt comfortable with, being too young, or the more abstract, "It's not the right time."'

## 4. Men at clinics

Peter said, 'I had the kids with me, so they made me wait outside with them. I felt really upset as I wanted to support Alice. I took the view it was her decision, but I'm still haunted by it.'

Gary said, 'I went along with Jeanette to the abortion clinic. The whole place was run by women. They apologised but said they only had time for women.'[7]

In America, about 600,000 men go to the abortion clinic every year with their female partners. 'Men and Abortion' is a website to give men a voice on abortion. About 6 in 10 men tend to be neutral but anxious before abortion. But afterwards some felt sad, lonely, guilty and powerless.[8]

Professor Arthur B. Shostak got interested after his own experience. He interviewed over a thousand men on their experience at the clinic. 'Overall, the impact seems to have promoted ever greater protective ambivalence – a stressful mix of anxiety ("Will she be okay?"), puzzlement ("How did we ever get into this mess?"), and resolve ("I never want to be here again, never!")'.

He goes on, 'Here is the shock of finding oneself unexpectedly in a no-nonsense "no second act" drama, whereby the well-being of a loved one (in most cases) is actually in jeopardy, and the well-being of a barely glimpsed stranger (the fetus) is being resolved emphatically – almost regardless of whatever feelings the male may have toward his supposed offspring.

'The sense of powerlessness is great and is aggravated by the loneliness of the men. Especially intriguing is the high percentage who report feeling guilty and sad.'[9]

Shostak showed that men wanted to talk. American clinics he surveyed had very few pamphlets available for men, yet men wanted counselling. When they questioned the clinics, most staff were female and unavailable for the men.

## 5. To save a relationship

Couples often choose abortion to save their relationship, but does it do that?

A psychotherapist answered the question this way: 'Unfortunately, all the evidence shows that abortion to "save a relationship" almost never works. Many relationships between couples come apart shortly after an abortion. These relationships often turn into prolonged, mutually destructive mourning rituals.'[10]

Even married couples are often driven apart by an abortion, unless they can find a way to complete the grieving process together.[11]

The anger generated spoils the joy of sex with failure or porn addiction. One young man reported, 'Sex became unpleasant or impossible.' Feelings can come out in vengeance sex so, 'Abortion breeds anger, resentment and bitterness toward the partner who was not supportive or who ignored their partner's desire to keep the baby.'[12]

13

## 6. Law and men

British law holds the man equally responsible with the woman for the child up to the age of 18. Yet, should the father want his unborn baby to be born he has no authority in the law. The choice is made by others. Since he feels emasculated by the law, the easy way out is abortion. At this point he may disappear from the scene since there is no child to protect and care for.

## 7. Conflict between men and women

Stories abound of women threatened into abortion or else... These powerful crosscurrents may break out in domestic violence – a huge issue which touch on in chapter 18 'Emotional and Mental After-effects'.

### So, who are the winners and losers?

• There is hope of a better long-term outcome for couples working hard at their relationship before, during and after pregnancy.

- Men don't feel the body chemistry and physical changes of a woman, but they can feel deeply affected by abortion loss for the rest of their lives.

- Fathers without legal rights in the decision can be left helpless – and this may backfire on his partner.

- Relationships in difficulty may worsen by abortion as the discord can divide partners and lead to loneliness, despair and suicide.

So, who are the winners and losers? Research suggests 8% of men feel deeply wounded, which is about 5 million in the States.[14] Estimates suggest some – perhaps many – men and women feel relieved in the short term, and perhaps even in the longer term. For others, the human costs fall heavily on both sides of the relationship which can spread to existing children and fracture other relationships.

## 8. Help and hope for men

There is help. The first step to recognise the damage can be the hardest of all. Mattes insists that healing is possible, and he wants the churches to be the first place for men to start. 'Men may feel no other crime can beat this one. But did not Jesus bleed and die even for this? There is no unforgivable sin.'

'Think of it like a spiral staircase,' says Mattes, 'where you climb slowly up towards the light that is filtering down from above.'

Men can be encouraged by hearing, 'You are not alone.' And it's good to act sooner rather than later.

See more in Appendix 2 'Finding Help' and at the Men and Abortion website.[15]

# Chapter 17
# Disability and Pre-birth Tests

As soon as you tell your doctor you are pregnant, you will probably get a question like, 'How do you feel about this pregnancy?' It's a way of getting you to think about whether you want a baby or an abortion.

However, it's understandable and normal to dread the idea of giving birth to a baby with serious physical or mental disabilities.

Abortion in the UK is now used for easily correctable problems, like cleft palate or clubfoot and numbers are rising.[1] This, and the growing number of prenatal tests, give parents-to-be a raft of dilemmas, not least, to test or not test?

**This chapter covers:**

1. Screening tests in pregnancy
2. NIPT (Non-invasive Pre-natal Testing)
3. Accuracy of diagnostic tests
4. We parents decide on testing – don't we?
5. What testing cannot do
6. Abortion for fetal disability – does it help?
7. Example: Down's syndrome
8. Finding help

We cover dilemmas where the child may be very much wanted, but parents face questions raised by antenatal screening and fears of disability.

Not everyone wants pre-natal testing. Here, you can find tips to partner with professionals and weigh the wisdom of screening tests on offer.

---

**Rio Williams**

Rio was born with Down's syndrome but is 'taking baby steps in an all new challenge;

**– modelling for Primark at 14 months'.**

Featured in Metro News UK, 3 April 2019

---

Picture perfect: Rio Williams is a natural in front of the lens as he poses with his mum Kimberly who is trying to change attitudes to Down's

**Rio Williams 2019[2]**

As before, we must always ask, 'Would abortion solve any problems – or add more?'

This chapter helps think that question through before you meet it in the antenatal clinic.

## 1. Screening tests in pregnancy

Thankfully, most babies are born without disability. The likelihood of having a major problem such as Down's syndrome, spina bifida or heart problem is about 4%.[3]

Abortion for disability accounts for about 1% of all British abortions – about 2,000 fetuses a year. But worryingly, 'Clear evidence now shows that the main influence on the woman's decision to abort is the "attitude of the health professional giving the counselling after diagnosis".'[4] This chapter will empower *you* to choose.

Screening has often changed the joy of an expected baby into an anxiety. Once the possibility of a 'wrong baby' is raised in parents it's hard to reassure them. This creates denial and distancing – so the ultrasound technician may hear, 'Don't show me the picture.'

Fetal screening is offered for a range of conditions, such as Down's syndrome, Edwards' syndrome and Patau's syndrome in the UK. A blood test called the 'combined test' is offered at 10 to 14 weeks into the pregnancy.

The screening blood test at 12-14 weeks will give your chances of your baby having Downs syndrome. You will be offered a more diagnostic test by the British NHS if the chance is above 1/150. This can be by a needle into the pregnancy for Chorionic Villous Sampling. The chance of miscarriage due to the needle is about 2/100. Errors can still happen so about one healthy baby is lost in order to find one unhealthy baby.[5]

The main thing that increases the chance of having a baby with Down's syndrome is the mother's age. For example, a woman who is:

- 20 years old has a 1 in 1,500 chance
- 30 years old has a 1 in 800 chance
- 35 years old has 1 in 270 chance
- 40 years old has a 1 in 100 chance, considered a 'small' chance by the NHS.[6]

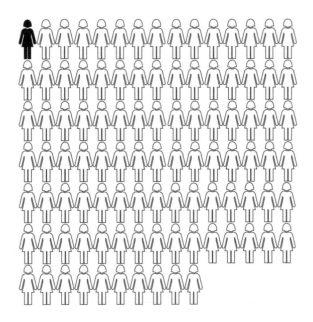

**Woman's risk of having a Down's syndrome child at age 40**

Spina bifida and other physical problems are screened at the 'Fetal Anomaly Scan' at about 20 weeks into pregnancy. Spina bifida is a defect in the spinal column and it can range from very minor, causing almost no problems, to major, with paralysis of the legs, bowels and waterworks. Women can take extra folic acid before and after conception to reduce the likelihood, as part of a healthy pregnancy diet. Amazing fetal surgery can now often correct it before birth.

While a mother may only want screening for reassurance that her baby is well, it is routine to discuss abortion if a problem is found. Sadly, the aim of reducing the suffering of parents-to-be by abortion can add years of suffering ahead, bring a new source of guilt and make closure hard to reach.

**There's a difference between 'screening tests' and 'diagnostic tests'.** Screening tests tell you the risk of your unborn having the problem being screened for – given as either a numerical risk such as: 1 in 100 or a description like, 'high risk' or 'low risk'.

A screening test cannot tell you that your unborn is *without* a problem, nor does it tell you the problem is *definitely* there. Despite 'precision' technology, it is not uncommon for false alarms to be raised. I have seen or heard of several cases locally in recent years, and we meet one of these later.

When the screening tests raise concern, then 'diagnostic tests' are offered to try and confirm or cancel the concern. In most pregnancies, these tests are used between weeks 11 and 25. In the much rarer, inherited diseases – 'in the family' – such as Huntingdon's disease, they can be done early after conception, or even before conception has occurred by gene studies.

Diagnostic tests can provoke unintended miscarriage. For example, for Chorionic Villus Sampling (CVS) or 'amniocentesis', the risk of losing the fetus is about one in 50 – and even then, the fetus may turn out to be healthy anyway.[7] It involves passing a needle into the placenta, through the mother's tummy or her vagina.

---

**How a couple made their choice**

'I was pregnant and we were worried because one screening test was abnormal; and we were about to get the result of the diagnostic test.

'Before we saw the doctor we talked it over with our pastor who said, "Decide what you're going to do with this baby *before* you get the result."

'As soon as the pastor said that we knew... "It's a no-brainer – we're going to have this baby whatever. So this diagnostic test will help us prepare beforehand to give her our best."'

---

## 2. NIPT (Non-invasive Pre-natal Testing)

This screening test looks at the genes. It is 'non-invasive' because it only needs a blood sample from a pregnant woman. Then they analyse the 'cell-free DNA' the genes floating in the mother's blood. Direct 'invasion' of the unborn and the risk of miscarriage is avoided.

NIPT is more accurate than other screening tests, but it can still be wrong. It's estimated that one-in-ten pregnant women with a high chance of Down's syndrome will have false positive from NIPT, where the baby in fact is healthy.[8] This generates anxiety in the parents who may then decide to opt for the invasive test like Chorionic Villous Sampling or go for an abortion.

In the UK, women found to have a higher chance of Down's syndrome screening tests are offered NIPT. It can find about 97% of fetuses with Down's syndrome.[9] It can also show the sex of the baby and syndromes like Edwards', Patau's, cystic fibrosis and achondroplasia, where these are in the family. Is it a 'search and destroy' process? Young people with Down's are becoming rare.

## 3. Accuracy of diagnostic tests

The routine ultrasound scan offered to all pregnant women in the UK, the 'fetal anomaly scan', is done at around 20 weeks. This test can be both a screening and a diagnostic test because it shows a high definition image of the baby.

How reliable is ultrasound to detect problems in the fetus:

- 'Incompatible with life' is 8 out of 10 attempts.
- 'Serious abnormalities' where survival is possible 5 out of 10.
- 'Requiring immediate care' after birth it is only about 2 out of 10.[10]

**Diagnostic tests for chromosome (gene) analysis** are 98–100% certain. However, the uncertainty comes with 'mosaic' gene patterns. Mosaic genes are a mixture of good and bad genes, making it hard to predict what the baby will be like when born.

## 4. We parents decide on testing – don't we?

Protecting your freedom of choice in the face of these mysterious tests can be difficult. Some couples refuse most screening tests. They say, 'Well, we plan to care for this baby anyway.'

The National Childbirth Trust (NCT) surveyed mothers' experiences of screening: 1 in 10 said they felt pressurised into having tests; they didn't feel the test for disability was presented as a choice.[11]

**If you choose the screening route,** here are some questions beforehand:

- Will this test make any difference to what we do in practice? Some test results can help prepare before birth for an abnormality. For instance, if the detailed physical scan at 20 weeks shows a marked cleft lip, which needs early help in feeding.
- If there's a problem, would we choose abortion? Is this a 'hunt and destroy' test, or are we seeing how the best can be done for all, including the unborn?
- If we choose abortion, how many aspects of the problem will that solve?
- Will abortion cure anything – or bring us more pain?
- Are we trying to achieve the perfect child for us and others to see?
- Older women may feel they have less chances to get pregnant, healthy or not. How is that for you?
- Have we exhausted all possible treatments for the condition in the fetus?
- What is the real problem? Is it the inner disappointment I feel? Is it the effort or expense of long-term care?
- Having dug down to the real problems, be they financial, personal cost, sense of shame or disappointment – what options have we to solve those?
- Are we using a minor abnormality as a cover for some other reason? For instance, are we really feeling that this pregnancy is just plain inconvenient?
- Will my partner and I feel that in a difficult situation we did the right thing and are content with that? (Chapter 16 'Men' explores the way relationships are affected by abortion decisions.)

The research into screening is disturbing showing that pregnancy is now anxious not joyful for 8 out of 10 women.[12]

**Taking charge of the screening decision**

To decide what testing you would like, think these questions listed above over beforehand. Jot them down (perhaps at the back of this book) and then talk it over with the midwife or doctor, who will usually go along with your wishes. Think about how you feel, when some 'experts' may think that even the possibility of a disability puts 'the good mother under a duty to abort'.[13] Who is the expert – you or the adviser who will not have to live with their choice? Most parents show an amazing desire and ability to care for a disabled baby.

**The positive side of screening**

If, sadly, a serious issue is found before birth, then the parents can do some grieving and the healthcare team can prepare to cope. Usually specialists can supply written and verbal information to prepare people for the expected problem. Very occasionally, this involves actual treatment of the fetus before birth – for instance surgery on spina bifida.

In a condition like anencephaly that has life expectancy measured in hours, due to major damage to the brain, delivery at the appropriate time can be arranged as part of planning terminal care for the baby, often in their mother's arms. Perinatal hospices have revolutionised such care while avoiding abortion or infanticide.

## 5. What testing cannot do

As said, prenatal testing cannot guarantee the right diagnosis is made and it cannot tell you how to choose. The kindly spoken, 'the abnormal baby is best aborted...' message may bring trouble long after, as experience has shown. That sort of decision, discovered using tools like the 4H in Part 1, comes from your Heart beliefs on life and death and exploring your options.

Two doctors, Annie and John (names changed), were expecting a baby. At their 18-week scan they heard that their baby probably had a major part missing from the brain. They were advised by a leading hospital in the UK that abortion was the best option.

After much thought they decided, 'We are not sure these tests are correct, and anyway, we don't want to abort.'

Their baby underwent several more tests, during which the abnormality was downgraded to 'a Down's syndrome like condition'.

They waited... At 40 weeks, the mother delivered a girl. The baby doctor examined Ivy carefully and announced, 'I think she is OK!'

She is now finishing primary school without problems.

**A correct diagnosis**

A couple were told that, sadly, their unborn had major disabilities and would live for only a few hours after birth.

They reluctantly decided to abort her early. Since then, they still grieve with complex feelings about the choice they made. Decades later, they still cannot easily discuss it.

## 6. Abortion for fetal disability – does it help?

Let's be aware of the enormous pain and desperation in these situations. Abortion may bring a sense of relief, mixed with the sadness. Yet, studies also show it brings a higher rate of depression in both mother and father; there may be guilt over what they have done. Added to this is the loss of self-esteem because they conceived an 'abnormal' baby. While there is no reason to feel guilty about this, nevertheless this false guilt feels so real.

Of course, having a disabled child can be devastating, and even break up a family. But it seems the long-lasting effects for some couples after ending a life can be greater.[14,15] The grief after these abortions can be as intense as for women suffering loss of a child near birth.[16]

## 7. Example: Down's syndrome

Hard as it may be to have a 'less-than-perfect' baby, the truth remains that every new life brings bonuses to our world. Down's syndrome is a useful example of this. A friend was helping at a toddler's crèche and told us:

Jimmy has Down's syndrome. 'When his mother came to collect him I said, "Jimmy has been happy and delightful to be with. But I'm afraid (smiling) two of the other toddlers have been howling non-stop whatever I do."

'"Oh, Jimmy is always easy," laughed the mum. "It's my other two that make me tear my hair out."'

---

Most people with Down's syndrome live fulfilled lives that contribute greatly to the community. Like other inherited problems, they come with a mix of mental and physical disabilities that means a lifetime of special care, yet videos testify to their happiness and careers they can fulfil.

Among parents of Down's, 99% reported they love their son or daughter; 97% were proud of them; 79% felt their outlook on life was more positive because of them; almost 90% of the siblings said they consider themselves better people because of their family member with Down's; 5% felt embarrassed by them and 4% regretted having them.'[17]

And don't we all need some special care to survive in life? It's just a question of how much. I have visited adults with Down's syndrome in their middle years leading contented lives in caring communities.

---

**Mohammed's story**

Mohammed and his wife have a little daughter, Sara, who has a condition like Down's syndrome. The couple are originally from a village in Pakistan.

'She is so special,' says Mohammed. 'When I put my shoes on to go out she says, "Da Da," and wants to come with me. She is without the jealousy of ordinary children, who say, "Hey, that's mine."

'She doesn't want to hurt anyone. All she needs is love. She gives to me something my other daughters don't give.'

With tears in his eyes, he goes on, 'In my country I knew a family of microcephalics [born with small heads]. We treated them as special people. They had something that others don't have. They were content with food and water, far more content than everyone else.'

Writing this chapter I am reminded of astonishing stories, like parents-to-be coping with long anxious weeks with great courage – weeks that turned to years. Or my cousin Peter and his wife Brigid and their boy Ben. Totally disabled and spending all day and night in bed, Ben was given four years to live. When he died in his twenties, the church funeral was packed with tearful people who saw significance in him and gained significance from him.

## 8. Finding help

Parents-to-be who have these tests and face a problem need much personal support. A life-affirming environment will help – a place where their child will be welcomed and supported with loving care and acceptance. Social groups like families and churches can provide this long-term.

Almost every problem has a website and groups to provide help and support.

# Part 3
# Informing Choice by Digging Deeper

## Introduction to Part 3

**Here is extra medical information.**

This is for professionals, policymakers and anyone wanting to dig deeper into medical evidence.

In unintended pregnancy, carers can take encouragement that proactive care of the pregnant woman helps prevent trouble later.[1] That's important since three systematic reviews show women with unintended pregnancy tend not to use antenatal services well; and they are at higher risk of preterm birth and perinatal depression.[2]

Most abortion research is difficult due to the understandable reluctance of women to reveal past abortion. Their feedback is further affected by whether they have or have not suffered serious life events later.

The public, and policymakers need to know that researchers are still obstructed by foot-dragging in England and the United States to link a woman's abortion history electronically with her long-term health outcomes.

However, other countries can do this, and we bring record linkage studies on whole nations that have unearthed important data for the health-rights and well-being of the public.

# Chapter 18
# Emotional and Mental After-effects

**This chapter covers:**

1. Introduction
2. Warning on mental health
3. A range of emotions
4. Suicide and pregnancy loss
5. Close relationship breakdown
6. Feeling suicidal?

## 1. Introduction

Most people agree abortion is unpleasant to go through. While many women feel short-term relief after the abortion, a concern is the longer-term mental health and peace of mind.

This chapter focuses largely on women, but men feel deeply the loss of their unborn and grieve silently and often destructively to themselves and those around. See chapter 16 'Men'.

People using abortion for severely abnormal babies are just as at risk as those seeking 'social or lifestyle abortion' – in fact they may be more at risk (see chapter 17 'Disability and Pre-birth Tests').

Talking over feelings with someone before deciding whether to have an abortion can help, and a pathway for this was outlined in Part 1 of this guide.

Abortion is promoted as a treatment or a choice to make women *feel better*. It may be justified legally (for instance in the UK) on the single ground that it will make a woman's *mental health better* compared to what it would be if she gave birth to a baby. This chapter examines those claims deeper than the Early and Later After-effects chapters.

As we saw in 'Later After-effects', Prof. David Fergusson concluded in a large study in 2013, that there is no available evidence that abortion has medical benefits.[1] Also, four researchers reported in 2017 that the emotional *benefits* of abortion have been little studied.[2]

And if no benefit, what about harm from abortion? Evidence is mounting of deep and long-term harm for women – harm like depression but also substance abuse, suicide, anxiety and PTSD (post-traumatic stress disorder). In young American women with mental disorders, investigated over a 13-year period, almost 1 in 10 of these mental problems were linked to earlier abortion (published 2016).[3]

## 2. Warning on mental health

Past or present mental health problems in a woman are a caution if she is considering abortion, because they raise her risk of major mental health problems afterwards.

A checklist of risk factors (American Psychological Association) is in chapter 13 'Early After-effects'.

## 3. A range of emotions

Most family doctors have seen women showing a range of emotions after abortion, from relief, to mild tearfulness, to extreme grief up to decades later. Some counsellors call it a loss that is difficult to talk about, 'a disenfranchised grief' because it's a choice the woman has made herself. There's the expectation that all should feel okay now that the abortion is done.

A study in 2016 of about 8,000 American women who were post-abortion and aged between 15 years old to 28 confirmed previous studies from Norway and New Zealand: abortion is consistently associated with increased risk of mental health disorder – including substance abuse.[4]

A major British review into mental health after abortion in 2011 found that having an 'unwanted' pregnancy is linked with increased risk of mental health problems. If the woman then goes on to have an abortion, this raised risk of mental health problem is *still there*.[5] So all women with an unwanted pregnancy need support and care, and it would be wrong to assume that abortion will solve a mental health problem whether related to the present pregnancy or not.

These cautions were supported by David Fergusson in 2013, who re-examined the British review. Fergusson was known to be pro-abortion. He with others found 'no available evidence to suggest that abortion has therapeutic effects in reducing the mental health risks of unwanted or unintended pregnancy. There is suggestive evidence that abortion may be associated with small to moderate increases in risks of some mental health problems', even in women with *no previous history of problems*.[6, 7]

Post-abortion counsellors report women with previously stable emotions plunging into deep distress afterwards that can be both immediate and last lifelong. While some women are glad of their abortion, the numbers and voices of those who are not deserve to be heard.

In contrast, no other pregnancy outcome, such as miscarriage or having a baby, were consistently linked to a raised risk of a mental health problem, except postnatal depression. This affects about 10 or 15 women in 100 before or after birth. The much milder 'baby blues' affect about half of all women in the first ten days after delivery. Tell your doctor if they persist for more than two weeks (advised by the Royal College of Psychiatrists 2018).[8]

The more severe *puerperal psychosis* following a birth affects about 1 woman in 1000 and can be life-threatening, needing urgent treatment. If the woman has a history of psychosis already, then she is at more risk of this re-occurring. Abortion, where there is a psychotic history, is contraindicated.[9, 10]

These major after-effects partly explain why women's deaths from suicides (six times higher) and other causes are higher in the years after abortion than the year after a birth. Researchers uncovered more deaths from domestic violence, strokes and road accidents contributing to why women die young in the years after abortion.[11]

## 4. Suicide and pregnancy loss

It has been known since the 1990s that unwanted pregnancy is itself a mental health risk. So, will having an abortion lower that risk?

Doctors studied this, and the bar charts showing the risks are under **Rate of attempted suicide per 1,000 young women** in chapter 15 'Teens – Special Care'.

While attempted suicide numbers are not the same as completed suicides, the authors of this *BMJ* study concluded, 'The increased risk of suicide after an induced abortion may therefore be a consequence of the procedure itself.'

## 5. Close relationship breakdown

While some couples look on their abortion as the right thing at the time, there is evidence that most relationships fail after abortion.[12, 13] The potential for inter-personal conflicts swells, reaching to the couple's parents, their existing children and children coming later.

For example, the woman may have felt she was not given a choice, while on the other hand the man can feel humiliated and bereaved – they argue and threaten. Then separation happens, the children suffer and loneliness in parents and children can lead to risky lifestyles and addictions.

Any breakdown of relationships tends to damage both parties emotionally and financially, especially the woman when she is most needing support. One testimony went, 'My husband started threatening me with separation if I did not agree to have an abortion... He kept yelling at me to sign the papers or abort the baby.' The authors of over 100 women's stories conclude: 'Healthcare professionals should be aware of the correlation between abuse and abortion... Far from eliminating abuse, an abortion can increase intimate partner violence.'[14]

Many couples sweep the abortion under the rug, but the emotional pain won't be ignored. They often vow to never speak of the 'event' again, but the other person is a daily reminder of what will never be. It can feel easier to end the relationship than face a painful and often hard-fought resolution – but it is worth the effort. (See also Appendix 2 'Finding Help'.)

## 6. Feeling suicidal?

Help is available for anxiety, shame, depression and loss, whether it's recent or a long time ago. A range of support groups, counselling and post-abortion programmes exist around the UK, Europe, North America and across the world.

Final healing may take time and persistence, and more than one type of professional help.

If you feel you cannot see a future, or you are...

---

**Feeling suicidal?**

**TELL SOMEONE YOU TRUST NOW**

(In the UK, dial 111 for the NHS)

---

# Chapter 19
# Infertility After Abortion

**This chapter draws together earlier information:**

1. What is infertility?
2. Risk of infertility after abortion
3. Why abortion can prevent a healthy child birth
4. Prevention

At the time of an unwanted pregnancy, a woman may not be concerned with having children, yet most people hope for a family one day. Before abortion, the professional's duty is to help her weigh threats to a successful live birth later.

Most abortions remove a healthy pregnancy; this delays future pregnancy, and with rising age and fertility falling rapidly through her thirties, the chances of a healthy child are dropping. Other factors stack up too.

## 1. What is infertility?

Strictly speaking infertility is the inability to achieve a pregnancy after 12 months of regular and unprotected sexual intercourse.[1] But here we cover any abortion complications which can impair hopes of a healthy baby later.

Overall, about 1 in 7 couples cannot conceive a pregnancy.[2] In about a third, the problem is related to the woman. That's 6.1 million women in the United States ages 15-44 having difficulty getting pregnant or staying pregnant.[3]

## 2. Risk of infertility after abortion

Women after abortion are 7 times more likely to have trouble conceiving.[4] A study from Shanghai in 2001 noted a significant association between fertility and previous abortion.[5] A Greek study showed abortion as an independent and significant risk to future fertility, with the risk increasing after a second abortion.[6]

### 3. Why abortion can prevent a healthy child birth

This summarises and supports the information in chapter 14 'Later After-effects' sections 3 and 4.

- **The woman cannot conceive** again (sub-fecundity).
- **Surgical damage to the cervix.**
- **Early miscarriage.**
- **Infection of the womb and fallopian tubes.** Infection can block the tubes so egg and sperm never meet for conception. Research from Washington State indicates 'a threefold elevated risk [of amniotic fluid infection] for both induced and spontaneous abortion with women after a prior livebirth. Our findings indicate that an abortion in a woman's first pregnancy does not have the same protective effect of lowering the risk for intrapartum infection in the following pregnancy as does a livebirth. Following an abortion after previous livebirth, there is a greater risk of infection of the womb and fallopian tubes.'[7]

## Fallopian tube obstruction

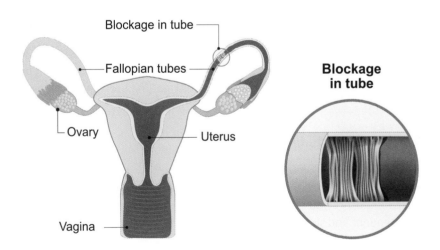

- **Ectopic pregnancy.** An Australian study found a woman's risk of ectopic pregnancy rises seven to ten times after infection and PID.[8] An Indian study put it at six times higher.[9] The sequence is that abortion leads to the pelvic infection which becomes PID and an ectopic pregnancy. One in 10 women who have PID will have an ectopic pregnancy.[10]
- **Stillbirth.**
- **Placenta praevia (PP).**
- **Preterm birth** (see chapters 14 and 29).
- **Early death of the mother,** associated with prior abortion, renders her unable to produce more children – thus bereaving and weakening the existing family.

Out of 101 women telling their abortion stories, among the 40 who answered the question on infertility, 23% reported they were unable to have children.[11]

By 2018, a Canadian team researching for 15 years concluded that 'evidence linking infertility to previous induced abortion is overwhelming'.[12]

# Chapter 20
# Premature Birth After Abortion

by Professor J. Wyatt and Dr Mark Houghton

**This chapter covers:**

1. What is a premature birth?
2. Abortion's link with premature birth
3. Why is preterm birth dangerous?
4. What factors increase the risk of preterm delivery?
5. Very preterm birth – extra dangers
6. Why should abortion raise the risk of later preterm delivery?
7. The main message

## 1. What is a premature birth?

A normal pregnancy lasts about nine months, or 40 weeks. When birth occurs before 37 weeks, it is defined technically as 'preterm' or 'premature,' 'prem' or 'preemie' for short. In the UK, about 7% of all births occur before 37 weeks. As you can see, their tiny size brings technical challenges to giving care.

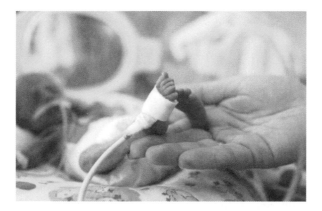

**A premature baby – to give an idea of their size**

## 2. Abortion's link with premature birth

Previous abortion has a strong statistical link with preterm birth in follow-on pregnancies, as the chart tracking abortion and preterm birth shows.[1] (Scotland can follow abortion outcomes using the NHS number linked on the abortion form – but England cannot.)

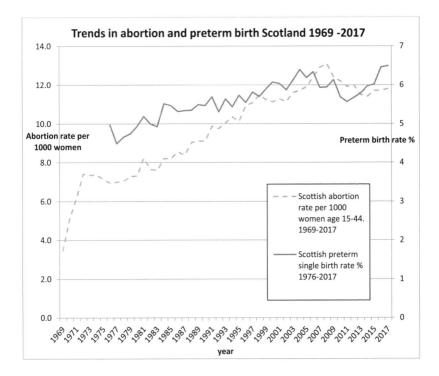

As expected, the rise in abortion rate needs a few years delay before showing the rise in preterm births.

The scientific evidence of a causal link between previous induced abortion and increased risk of preterm delivery appears to be very robust and consistent. The effect is consistent across studies published over a 50-year period from the 1960s to the present. It is consistent in studies involving many different countries with widely differing socioeconomic backgrounds and widely differing attitudes towards induced abortion.

## 3. Why is preterm birth dangerous?

The more preterm a baby is at the time of birth, the more likely they are to have problems in the first days and weeks of life, because of the immaturity of their organs.

Babies born before 32 weeks – 'very preterm' – account for about 1% of all births in the UK. These babies are likely to require treatment in hospital for weeks or, sadly, can die. They have an increased risk of complications, particularly from immature lungs and brain. Brain bleeding injury is a major concern because it may have long-term effects, including cerebral palsy, learning difficulties, and behavioural challenges including autistic spectrum disorder.

The greatest risk is with babies born at the limits of continuing life – those born around 22–25 weeks. The numbers are relatively small (about 2 per 1,000 births in the UK) but unfortunately, they have a high risk of death immediately after birth. Between a quarter to a half (20% and 50%) of babies will die before discharge from hospital, and half of those who survive have a high risk (up to 50%) of some permanent brain injury.[2, 3]

## 4. What factors increase the risk of preterm delivery?

Many studies have searched for why a mother will go into labour early and deliver a premature baby. Medically these include infection, an abnormally shaped womb and high blood pressure in the mother. Social factors like deprivation and domestic abuse can provoke preterm labour, as can previous abortion.

A strong and consistent link has been found between a previous induced abortion and an increased risk of preterm delivery in a subsequent pregnancy. There is a 30%–60% increased risk of preterm delivery following a previous induced abortion.

There are statistical methods for adjusting the figures to consider known risk factors for prematurity. Considering the other conditions like those listed above, a study combining 37 other studies (meta-analysis) found that one previous induced abortion made a preterm birth 27% (about a third) more likely than full-term pregnancy. Two or more previous abortions made preterm birth 62% (about two thirds) more likely.[4] Another meta-analysis published in 2016 found a raised risk of premature birth after two or more surgical abortions.[5]

What are these studies showing? The more abortions a woman has, the more likely it is that she will have a premature baby from a later pregnancy. Harvard University found Black American women more than double their future preterm risk after more than one abortion compared to Black American women without prior abortion.[6]

So, it is fair to say that a strong scientific link exists between abortion and preterm delivery of a next baby.

## 5. Very preterm birth – extra dangers

Very preterm birth (and extremely preterm birth) are the most dangerous of all to the infant. Studies show the risk of 'very preterm' delivery (below 32 weeks) is significantly increased after a previous induced abortion. A meta-analysis (study of 12 studies) in 2009 found that women who'd had one or more previous induced abortions had on average a *64% higher risk* of a very preterm delivery compared to women with no previous abortions.[7] Women with a history of induced abortion were at higher risk of very preterm delivery than those with no such history (OR + 1.5, 95% CI 1.1-2.0); the risk was even higher for extremely preterm deliveries (less than 28 weeks).[8]

Sadly, as we go to press the fullest study of world literature so far will show a five times increased risk of *very preterm birth* after 3 or more abortions – the very ones at the most risk of dying or of long-term and permanent after-effects.[9]

This is supported by a registry study from Finland by Klemetti et al. – quoted on the British NHS Choices health enquiry website – who also found increased risk of very preterm birth under 28 weeks with unadjusted odds ratio of 1.22 for 1 abortion, 1.86 for 2 abortions, and 3.38 after 3 or more abortions.[10]

## 6. Why should abortion raise the risk of later preterm delivery?

Several known biological factors can explain the link between abortion and subsequent preterm delivery. For instance, there is strong evidence that induced abortion increases the risk of complications from infection in a later pregnancy, and it is well known that pelvic infection and chronic pelvic inflammatory disease (PID) increase the risk of subsequent preterm delivery.[11]

This results from hidden infection caused by surgical trauma to tissues at the time of the abortion. Surgical abortion may injure the cervix making it vulnerable to infection. This is a well-known cause of subsequent preterm delivery.

Surgical instruments inserted at abortion may damage the lining of the womb, interfering with normal positioning of the placenta. This would increase the risk of placenta praevia. Placenta praevia is at risk of serious bleeding and a well known risk for preterm birth.

Studies have shown a consistent statistical relationship between induced abortion and subsequent preterm delivery due to infection or cervical problems, but not between abortion and preterm delivery resulting from other factors like high blood pressure in the mother. This provides further support for what we suspect – that it is the abortion itself which is adding to the increased risk of having a preterm baby in a later pregnancy.[12]

## 7. The main message

Most people are unaware of this clear connection between induced abortion and an increased risk of preterm delivery in follow-on pregnancies. Based on published data, approximately 14% of all women in the UK who deliver have already had an abortion.[13]

So, using this figure above and recent research that there is an increased risk of 30% for very preterm birth, it can be calculated that previous abortion is leading to *325 more* very preterm babies born before 32 weeks every year in the UK.

In addition, we can expect more than *245 'extremely preterm'* births, born earlier than 28 weeks.

---

Together these make almost **700 additional premature** babies born in the UK every year from a known and avoidable cause.

---

The financial cost to the nation is billions of pounds needed in care. Who can calculate the human cost to the parents, the families and the children themselves – some becoming disabled adults?[14]

Approximately half of all abortions in England and Wales are undertaken in women under the age of 25 years, whereas three quarters of all live births occur in mothers over the age of 25. Most of the women who are considering abortion will later deliver one or more children.

It is *essential* that women and their partners are adequately informed about the possible effects of abortion on them and follow-on children.

• **In the United States** researchers calculated that in a year, prior induced abortions led to over 1,000 cases of cerebral palsy because of babies born prematurely. Induced abortion contributes to significantly increased neonatal health costs by causing 31.5% of extremely preterm births.[15]

## Ball park figures:

• Two abortions double the preterm risk.
• Three abortions triple the risk (new evidence will show 5 times higher).

It is this group of infants that are sadly most likely to die in the first days and weeks after birth. Survivors carry a significant risk of brain damage leading to cerebral palsy and challenging behaviour.

# Chapter 21
# Breast Cancer After Abortion?

*'Cutting a pregnancy off early, under 32 weeks, leaves the woman permanently with breasts in a cancer prone state.'*[1]

(Dr Mary L. Davenport, MD, Vice President,
Breast Cancer Prevention Institute)

**This chapter covers:**

1. How many women?
2. The key factor
3. Abortion following a birth – what's the risk of cancer?
4. Repeat abortions raise cancer risk
5. Other lifestyle factors fuelling the rise
6. Why is the abortion–breast cancer link not better known?
7. But some studies show childbirth is more risky
8. The biological reasons for the link
9. Healthy Irish women have fewer breast cancers
10. Errors in a major US report, March 2018
11. Association or causation?
12. In conclusion

## 1. How many women?

**In the USA,** abortion was legalised in 1973 and the breast cancer incidence has risen since 1975. The cumulative lifetime risk has risen from 1 in 12 to 1 in 8 women since 1975.

**In the UK,** female breast cancer is the commonest cancer in women and rising since legalisation of mass abortion in 1968.

- In females in the UK, there were around 54,500 new cases in 2016 – that's like London's Wembley Stadium over half-full of women.
- Breast cancer is the most common cancer in the UK, accounting for 15% of all new cancer cases (2016).

- Since the early 1990s, breast cancer incidence rates have increased by a fifth (20%) in the UK in females.
- These happen most often in women between the ages of 15 and 60 years.[2]

Thankfully, about 85% of those are expected to survive for at least five years with expert care.[3]

The risk of a British woman getting malignant breast cancer in her lifetime was about 1 in 8, but by 2017 this had risen to about 1 in 7 women (lower risks in Northern Ireland). If one counts women with pre-cancer changes (that's carcinoma in situ – which is early cancer) it's close to 1 in 6 women.[4]

Since 1983 the breast cancer incidence rose across China, a brief lag behind abortion. The respected Dr Lei Fan said, 'Incidence increased dramatically over the past 30 years... a 20–30% increase over the past decade [to 2009]... Birth control policies [the one child policy since 1979] have... pushed the pattern of breast cancer in Shanghai towards that of the western countries.'[5]

Romania, the USSR, India, Bangladesh, Sri Lanka and Pakistan show similar patterns.

## 2. The key factor

As we saw in Part 2, the *key risk factor* for breast cancer is her age of first full-term pregnancy (FFTP).[6]

Also at risk are women aged 50 to 100 who had an abortion when young, especially if it delayed their first full-term pregnancy.

Modern studies on this age of first full-term pregnancy factor have been accepted science for decades. Back in 1983 Trichopolous, studying 17,000 women, showed that every five years' delay in FFTP associated with nearly one-fifth increase in risk of breast cancer.[7]

---

Each five-year delay in FFTP

adds one-fifth higher risk of breast cancer.[8]

---

The Trichopolous authors said, 'There is evidence that the age of approximately 35 years represents for every birth a critical point; before this age any full-term pregnancy confers some degree of protection; which is further increased by breastfeeding [which cannot happen if the pregnancy is aborted] and avoiding the hormonal contraceptive pill.'[9]

> Doubling the woman's age delay from five years to ten years later for her FFTP roughly doubles her increase in breast cancer risk over her lifetime.[10]

### Digging deeper into Annie's breast cancer causation

Earlier, in the 'Later After-effects' chapter, we met Annie discovering her breast lump 30 years since her abortion in her twenties. It would be reasonable to ask, 'Perhaps her breast cancer risk was only higher because she was older when her first baby arrived? After all, the longer she lives, the more time available to be unlucky and get cancer.'

No, this is probably not the case. There are four *independent* risk factors explaining why delay in FFTP by abortion can be linked to higher risk of breast cancer:

- Annie is older when she has her first full-term pregnancy.
- Annie missed out on the chance to protect her breasts by feeding her child in her teens.[11]
- Annie is interrupting her pregnancy in the first trimester (first 12 weeks).
- Annie raised her risk of premature birth (born before 32 weeks) in her following pregnancies. Prem birth is an independent risk factor for breast cancer. This was shown by Melbye (1999) who is well known in this field and several other papers.[12] They wrote, 'An abortion can be thought of as premature delivery by an abortionist, such that premature delivery before 32 weeks doubles the breast cancer risk because the breasts are left with more lobules where breast cancers can start.'

**Miscarriage.** If she loses the baby through miscarriage in the first 12 weeks, then she *does not suffer such a large rise* in risk of later breast cancer as having an abortion. (However, miscarriage in the middle trimester of pregnancy *does* carry a higher risk of breast cancer because middle trimester miscarriages have normal hormone levels. The cause then may be the umbilical cord wound around the neck or other accidents.)

Early miscarriages can happen in women who have low oestrogen (estrogen) hormone; having low oestrogen means fewer breast cells change to the high-risk state. In a study by Kunz and P.J. Keller they found: women who spotted blood while pregnant tended to have miscarriages if their oestrogen levels were found to be low.[13] If their oestrogen levels were normal, they were less prone to miscarry.[14]

## 3. Abortion following a birth – what's the risk of cancer?

New evidence from India and China shows that even in women who had their FFTP when young, an abortion will still cause a higher cancer risk for her lifetime.[15] A meta-analysis of 36 studies by Huang et al. in 2014 had already highlighted this.[16] Huang said their results were consistent with Brind's previously published systematic review in 1996. Huang found one abortion raised the risk by as much as 44%.

**Medical abortion higher risk?** A Chinese study published as we go to press suggests chemical *may* be much worse than surgical abortion regarding breast cancer risk.[17]

British specialists were recently still reassuring people that there is no abortion–breast cancer (ABC) link, but this is often based on a study from 2004 by Beral.[18] In the ten years of research from 2006 to 2016 there were 46 peer-reviewed scientific studies involving the ABC link. All, except one study, found that previous abortions raise the breast cancer risk.[19]

Back further, from 1957 to 2018 there are 76 studies differentiating induced from spontaneous abortion (miscarriage). Of these 76, there were 60 studies showing a positive association and 36 studies are statistically significant to the 95th percentile.[20]

**For each year a woman delays her pregnancy after age 20:**

- She increases her risk of premenopausal breast cancer (the more dangerous one) by 5% per year.
- Post-menopausal breast cancer 3% per year.[21]

## 4. Repeat abortions raise cancer risk

Huang's 2014 meta-analysis also showed the more abortions a woman has, the greater her risk of breast cancer – the 'dose effect'.[22]

Another Chinese study in 2012 showed the 'dose response' phenomenon, with two abortions being riskier than one. They found that women who had had one previous abortion experienced a 33% increase risk for one abortion, 76% for two abortions and 165% for three or more abortions.[23]

The 2001 Henriet study on French women who'd had more than one previous abortion also showed their risk of cancer roughly doubles after the age of 34 years. This is partially due to them being older first-time mothers, who are already at higher risk.[24]

## 5. Other lifestyle factors fuelling the rise

Hormones seem to be the most important cause of cancer change in her breasts. That's why the following factors can also increase your risk:

- The older you are at the time of your FFTP.
- Starting your periods early in life.
- Breastfeeding a baby is protective against breast cancer and the longer the better.
- Hormone replacement therapy (HRT) and the oral contraceptive pill both bring a similar higher relative risk of breast cancer. A woman's risk doubles with either of these, so that by the age of 50, her risk of breast cancer rises to 1 in 25 women not 1 in 50.[25] The lifetime risk is much higher again, at 1 in 6 or 1 in 7, as we saw at the start of the chapter.
- Family history. About 5–10% of women inherit a gene that is linked to breast cancer which needs specialist genetic advice.

### 6. Why is the ABC link not better known?

Leaving aside commercial interests, British doctors are still much influenced by Beral's study back in 2004.[26] However, errors in her methods have been publicised (including in the British Parliament in 2007).[27]

Firstly, Beral's team overlooked the fact that women can lower their breast cancer risk by breastfeeding[28] – if women have an abortion, the protective period of breastfeeding is lost.

Secondly, they overlooked the accepted research that the older the woman is at FFTP, the higher her risk of breast cancer.

Thirdly, Beral was quoted as saying, 'Scientifically this is a full analysis of the current data.'[29] Yet, important studies were left out and unreliable studies put in.[30] The American report of 2018 has serious errors also, see later.

## 7. But some studies show childbirth is more risky

A report in 2018 claimed that childbirth *increases* breast cancer risk for another 24 years after. However, the researcher had failed to include whether the women studied had had a past abortion. This, of course, changed the whole study![31]

In fact, there is a *temporary* association between childbirth and a rise in breast cancer risk – temporary because it is only for those who have *first childbirth* after 25, and the effect wears off by 40. This finding may be due partly to a weakness of that research in that past abortions were not allowed for in the Nicholls study.[32]

**Double-edged sword.** The Melbye study showed women who get pregnant at 20 have an immediate reduction in risk, but women who get pregnant at 35 initially have a 40% increase in risk which diminishes over 15 years until they get the benefit of risk reduction for life. This chart shows the data.

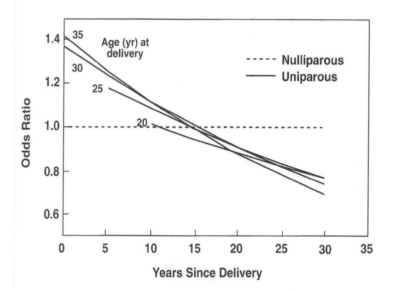

**Double-edged Sword: The Risk of Breast Cancer at Age of Delivery[33]**

(Nulliparous women are those who never gave birth. Uniparous is women who gave birth once.)[34]

## 8. The biological reasons for the link[35]

The protective effect of a full-term pregnancy on breast cancer risk has been known since the Middle Ages. Later in the eighteenth century, Ramazzinni of Padua (1743) reported that Italian nuns who had never been pregnant were more likely to get breast cancer.

Today we know the molecular basis of protective effects of a full-term pregnancy. For instance, the breast cells change and multiply when a woman is pregnant and getting ready to provide milk for a baby, which is why breasts get bigger during pregnancy. Breast duct cell cancers account for 85% of all cancers. In the first half of pregnancy this new breast tissue (Type 1 and 2 lobules) is vulnerable to cancer – but only for a time – because another change happens through pregnancy putting the cells in a safer state than before the woman was pregnant, as the table shows.

**Table: Breast Tissue Changes through Life[36]**

A lobule is a unit of breast tissue composed of a milk duct with its surrounding mammary (milk) glands, which are both composed of individual breast cells.

| Breast development | State of breast lobule |
|---|---|
| After puberty and before first pregnancy | Cells are 75% Type 1 and 25% Type 2 lobules (both types are cancer prone). |
| After conceiving a pregnancy | The Type 1 and Type 2 lobules increase. |
| By 20 weeks gestation | A great increase in the Type 1 and Type 2 lobules has happened; maturing into Type 4 lobules (cancer safe) has begun. |
| By 32 Weeks gestation | Enough Type 1 and 2 lobules have matured into Type 4 to lower the risk of breast cancer for the rest of her life. |
| By 40 weeks gestation | Now 70 to 90% of the breast tissue is cancer resistant. |
| After weaning | Type 4 lobules regress to Type 3 cells which have permanent genetic changes resistant to cancer. |
| After menopause | Type 3 lobules have changed again to look like Type 1 but for unknown reasons the genes do not change their regulation and the lobules remain cancer resistant. |

In the second half of pregnancy, the cells undergo maturation to Type 4 lobules where full terminal differentiation confers cancer protection. Many cancers originate in stem cells in the breast. Having a full-term pregnancy reduces the number of stem cells in the breast, thereby reducing breast cancer risk.[37]

A young woman who has never been pregnant has breasts which are already more prone to develop a cancer. Early pregnancy then makes the breasts even more cancer-prone by stimulating the multiplying of Type 1 and 2 lobules.

**The breasts diagram below** shows the changes from before her first pregnancy till after abortion of that pregnancy.

The *darker* cells nearest to the nipple, called Type 1 lobules, produce 80% of later cancers (Ductular type). In the right-hand picture these have multiplied by the time pregnancy ends due to abortion.[38]

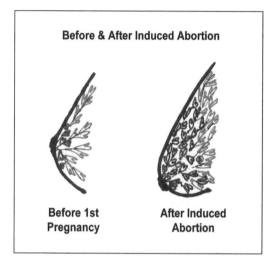

**Before & After Induced Abortion**

Before 1st
Pregnancy

After Induced
Abortion

**The right-hand picture** above, After Induced Abortion, shows how the Type 2 lobules (furthest from the nipple) – have also multiplied in the first few weeks of pregnancy. Most abortions cut off any further cell changes at this stage. Type 2 lobules account for 15% of later cancers (Lobular type).

However, continuing pregnancy by avoiding abortion matures these high-risk cells into a lower-risk state as this table shows:

| Timing | Lobules | Other tissues |
|---|---|---|
| **First half of pregnancy** | Type 1 and 2 lobules increase which doubles the breast volume.<br><br>These are both cancer prone. | Decrease in the fatty and connective tissues. |
| **Second half of pregnancy** | Slow down in the proliferation of new cells.<br><br>Conversion into Type 3 lobules.<br><br>Lobules mature into Type 4. | Milk creation is inhibited until birth by hormones from the placenta. |

**Table of Breast Tissue Changes in Pregnancy[39]**

There is a critical duration to achieve this change and it is those first 32 weeks of pregnancy. So long as she gets *beyond 32* weeks, the cancer-prone breast tissue has a chance to mature into cancer-resistant Type 3 and 4 lobules. This is because around this time the fetus and placenta produce 'human placental lactogen' (HPL), which helps breast cells become cancer-resistant. This explains why women who give birth prematurely before 32 weeks are at higher risk of breast cancer later.

Any pregnancy that ends before 32 weeks, through premature birth or abortion, stops this tissue change from completing; the woman is left with breast tissue that has become even more at risk of becoming cancerous than if she had never been pregnant at all. These cells remain cancer vulnerable for the rest of her life. Clearly abortion cannot remove these cells.[40]

*'Cutting a pregnancy off early, under 32 weeks, leaves the woman permanently with breasts in a cancer prone state.'*

**If the woman breastfeeds** her baby, then her cancer protection is increased even more than the protection of having a full-term birth. That's because not until lactation do CK8/18 stem cells undergo terminal differentiation to become secretory end cells. Terminally differentiated cells do not form cancer.[41]

### How pregnancy hormones change the breast tissue

During pregnancy, hormones such as oestrogen, which stimulates breast cancer cells, have been released around the body in larger quantities than before the pregnancy. The NHS website states, 'The hormone oestrogen is responsible for almost all breast cancer risks in one way or another.'[42]

## 9. Healthy Irish women have fewer breast cancers

Whole nations can benefit. In 2017, the *Journal of American Physicians and Surgeons* showed that abortion was the greatest predictor of breast cancer frequency in nine European countries: England, Wales, Scotland, Northern Ireland, the Irish Republic, Sweden, the Czech Republic, Finland and Denmark.[43]

Irish women have been shown to have lower risks of breast cancer, at 1 woman in 10 before the age of 75,[44] than women in England and Wales.[45]

Until the Irish liberalised abortion law in 2018, fewer Irish women had abortions than England and Wales, and the Northern Irish women less than those in the Republic.

Since 1968, when abortion numbers in England and Wales soared, English and Welsh women suffered a parallel increase (but delayed by some years) in breast cancer rates, [46, 47] while there was a much lower rise in rates of breast cancer in Irish women. Remember, there will be a time-lag before the increase in abortions shows up in cancer rates.

'The correlation is very high between cumulated cohort rates of abortion and cumulated cohort breast cancer incidence rates in all the countries with good records of both episodes. This is evidence.' (Patrick Carroll, Statistician) [48, 49]

On the other hand, the more full-term pregnancies a woman has, the more protected she is from developing breast cancer. A Swedish study in 1996 showed that each baby born lowers a woman's risk of breast cancer by another 10%. [50]

## 10.  Errors in a major US report, March 2018[51]

'The Safety and Quality of Abortion Care in the United States', from the National Academies of Sciences (NAS), is a single page relying on three studies done after 2000. They conclude there is no risk of breast cancer after abortion. They ignore the accepted and well-known facts mentioned above.

But the three studies they chose were Newcomb 2000, Goldacre 2001 and Brewster 2005. Thus, they eliminate the 25 statistically significant studies done from 1957 to 1999.

The Newcomb study had only 23 women with an abortion history. The authors caution, 'Some limitations of this study should be considered in interpreting our results.'

In the Goldacre study, even the authors state, 'Our data on abortions are substantially incomplete because they only include women admitted to hospital, and only include those in the care of the NHS (UK public healthcare).' Only 300 were classified as having a history of induced abortion – barely 1% over a 30-year period of abortions done in the UK, whereas about 33% of British women have had abortion by 50 (excluding Northern Ireland).

In the Brewster study, the authors admit, 'The important weakness of the study relates to missing data on miscarriage and induced abortion and potential confounding factors for a substantial proportion of the original study population.'

'Recall bias' is a problem in these studies. Recall bias means women without cancer will underreport (deny) abortions, while those women with cancer will admit to abortions. The NAS impugned case-control studies with recall/reporting bias. Yet when looked for in studies, the reality of recall bias could not be verified.

## 11. Association or causation?

We cannot say 'causes' between two events, for instance smoking and lung cancer, *unless the evidence meets the Bradford Hill criteria*. The arguments for causation between abortion and breast cancer in a woman fulfil the nine positive Bradford Hill criteria, including the sound biological explanation mentioned above.[52]

a. Timing: the patient must be exposed to the risk before the cancer.
b. Similar findings in many studies: 60/76 studies worldwide; 19/24 in the US associate abortion and breast cancer.
c. Statistically significant increase in risk: 36 studies worldwide; 9 US studies are statistically significant.
d. Dose effect: the risk should rise with more exposure to the risk. The longer the pregnancy before abortion, or the more abortions, the higher the risk. For instance see the 1994 Dayling study and 1997 Mebye study.
e. A large effect observed with Relative Risk greater than 3. See the Dayling study 1994 with the subgroup of teens showing an 800% increased risk in 18 years old and younger. Also women over 30 and family history all have over 200% increased risk.
f. Causal association is biologically plausible (see above).
g. Experimental studies: Russo and Russo experimented on virgin and aborted rats and rats who gave birth at term. The aborted rats showed the greatest changes (1980).
h. Coherence in the natural history and biology of breast cancer: the breast cancers caused by abortion appear after 8 to 14 years and average cancer cell growth takes 8 to 10 years to be clinically detectable.
i. Analogy — similar exposures are associated with similar effects: if

there is premature delivery before 32 weeks for another reason than abortion, one still finds the breast cancer risk doubles.

---

**Black-American women**

A 2017 study found that Black-American women who breastfeed over 11 months cut their triple negative breast cancer odds by nearly half.[53]

---

## 12. In conclusion

Abortion is not the only factor in the rise of breast cancer in the last 50 years, but there is overwhelming evidence of the link. And not only a link but cause and effect. There is no doubt this debate must continue because women's lives, clinical decision-making, and legal rulings rest on this evidence.

# Chapter 22
# Mortality of Women

As we saw (chapter 14), large Scandinavian studies show women dying young, average age 28, associated with previous abortion.

These are 3 to 4 times higher rates of early death than if they gave birth. So, imagine two Wembley Stadiums in London full of 200,000 British women (which is the number having abortions every year) we lose around 100 additional women every year, many leaving motherless families.

**This chapter covers:**

1. The evidence
2. Danish women's lives and deaths
3. Californian women
4. Benefits of birth
5. Finnish women's one-year risk
6. Danish women's six-fold benefit
7. Suicides – don't despair
8. Why the women die
9. Tighter abortion laws *safer* for women
10. In conclusion

## 1. The evidence

Denmark and Finland have excellent abortion records from 1973 and 1983 respectively. A woman's whole life can be followed from birth to death and linked with her abortion history. This gets around the mortality definition issues and the failures in countries like the USA and England that don't allow abortion records to be linked up with their deaths. Such anti-woman discrimination provoked questions in parliament in 2018.[1]

## 2. Danish women's lives and deaths

Here's how 463,000 Danish women fared in the ten years after either birth or abortion (up to 12 weeks).[2]

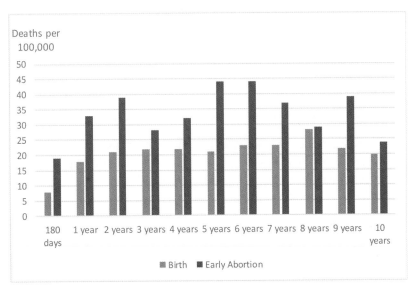

**Women's mortality rates following first pregnancy outcome at 180 days and during each of first to tenth years after pregnancy ends.**

(Data points from Reardon DC, Coleman PK. Short and long-term mortality rates associated with first pregnancy outcome: population register based study for Denmark 1980-2004. *Med Sci Monit.* 2012;18(9): PH71 PH76. Table 1 with 180-day data from Table 2.)

## Women's deaths for 10 years after birth or early abortion.

(This study did not control for social and financial factors, marital status or mental health before the abortion.)

Women who ended their first pregnancy with an early abortion had significantly higher mortality rates year-on-year for ten years (the same was true for late abortion, though this is not shown in the chart above).[3]

The women's average age of early death was 27 years.

## 3. Californian women

Another study from California confirms this mortality risk. It looked at eight years of a woman's life after abortion compared to birth.

**Birth after abortion almost halves her risk** at 462 per 100,000 over 8 years, while for women who had abortions during the same time frame, 854 deaths per 100,000, or about double the risk.[4]

The average age of death was 28 years.[5]

None of this is new. In the US, back in 1985, induced abortion was the fifth leading cause of maternal mortality. This was the case even though these abortion statistics excluded suicide, avoidable deaths from injuries, accidents, substance abuse and contributory cumulative disease states – any of which might also be abortion linked and raise the true numbers higher.[6]

## 4.  Benefits of birth

Encouragingly for women, these Californian, Danish and Finnish studies suggest birth after previous abortion helps reduce their higher risk of dying. Pregnancy, birth and babies do one good.

## 5.  Finnish women's one-year risk

A study on one million Finnish women (2004)[7] also showed their mortality was 3 times lower in the year after a birth (28.2 deaths/100,000 pregnant women) than in the year after abortion (83.1 deaths/100,000 pregnant women) after adjusting for age. Mika Gissler showed miscarriage was in between (56 deaths/100,000 women). That's similar to Gissler's work quoted in chapter 14.

**One year deaths per
100,000 women**

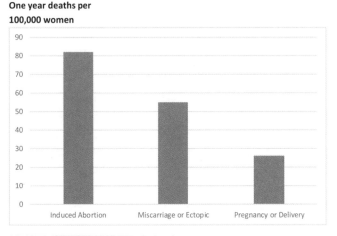

**Pregnancy associated death rates by pregnancy outcome, combining deaths during pregnancy and within one year of a term delivery**

### 1 Year Mortality after Abortion, Miscarriage or Birth[8]

## 6. Danish women's six-fold benefit

Those one million Danish women we 'met' (chapter 14, section 6) were followed 25 years after pregnancy ended. Their survival chances were 6 times better if they chose births (and had no natural miscarriages) than *those never pregnant.*

## 7. Suicides – don't despair

We are here to help. If you feel low or like ending it all there is help and hope (see back of this guide).

In general pregnancy loss from any cause can raise suicide risks adding to overall mortality compared to giving birth. [9,10] (More in chapters, 'Emotional and Mental After-effects' and 'Teenagers – Special Care'.)

## 8. Why the women die

Why should abortion be linked to deaths in women? The risks were mainly from 'outside' causes such as suicide, murder and accidents – including more road traffic accidents linked to risk-taking behaviour – rather than 'internal' causes like bleeding or infection.[11, 12, 13]

Some died of high blood pressure and strokes. Could these lethal events be stress-related following the pregnancy loss?[14, 15]

## 9. Tighter abortion laws safer for women

Are women at risk of more birth-related deaths where abortion is illegal? One would think so. But, Chile banned abortion in 1999 and this was studied by Koch et al. who found, 'Prohibition of abortion in Chile did not influence the downward trend in the maternal mortality ratio. Thus, the legal status of abortion does not appear to be related to overall rates of maternal mortality [using multivariable analysis].'[16]

They found women's mortality was best reduced by *schooling* of the mother. When challenged by another study, they were able to replicate their findings in a Mexican study.[17] In addition, Koch looked at 11 determinants of maternal mortality and found seven factors – the top three benefits being:

- Schooling for the mother – 30% reduction
- Access to emergency care – 30% reduction
- Skilled attendants at her birth – 20% reduction

## 10. In conclusion

These studies display the risks to a woman's life in the years after abortion. A 2017 meta-analysis reinforces the findings.[18] Remembering the women who have come to us far beyond this 25 years, we believe risks to life from suicide last much longer.

Repeat abortions have a 'dose effect', raising the deaths two to three times higher than having a baby.

These women might have decided to give birth had they known the better chances of being alive longer.

Over the next 8 years our nation will lose around 800 women who would be alive. These are *healthy* women (because sick women don't need abortion).

---

**Women deserve** to be given the benefit of examining this research and to make their own decisions about it.

---

# Appendix 1
# ABC of Spiritual Beliefs

Love, sympathy and hope can do wonders in any situation including a problem pregnancy, before or after an abortion. But is more needed?

Some go through these dilemmas and apparently feel fine. But stories from women and pastors, doctors and counsellors show many feel differently and have deep questions and suffering.

> 49-year-old Dr Adams sat at her desk after a long day. The last patient was gone, and she scratched her head, wondering, 'Why am I still so troubled by that abortion I did when I was 29?'

What can the great world faiths offer a person for that? Pregnancy and abortion raise questions, such as: When does life begin... or end? How can I handle my situation? Why do I regret what I have done? Why the shame and fear? Who has some answers?

**This chapter covers:**

1. What is a worldview?
2. Atheism
3. Buddhism
4. Christianity
5. Hinduism
6. Islam
7. Judaism
8. Sikhism
9. To make mistakes is to be human

## 1.  What is a worldview?

While science helps us know true and false in the physical world, it is almost powerless for issues of the human heart – what's the meaning of life and death, right and wrong – and people who regained a clear conscience – how did they do that?

These heart beliefs make up our 'worldview' and steer many practical choices in life. The General Medical Council (GMC) in the UK affirms the importance of the doctor knowing and respecting the patient's worldview.

---

**What's your worldview?**

Your worldview is your set of beliefs about aspects of reality, about where you came from, why you are here and what happens when you die. It is your view of the world, morality and the universe.

---

Life and coping with its difficulties go easier when decisions agree with inner values.[1] Some call these our 'conscience'. Several values are found in all cultures and even political groups around the world, values like freedom and fairness are among the strongest.[2]

**The ABC of beliefs** looks at the major faiths about life, how they view abortion and how they might help if one has regrets.

Professor Richard Vincent, first Dean of Brighton Medical School, reminds people that out of 1,200 scientific studies on faith in healthcare, 81% show benefit and 4% harm.[3]

## 2. Atheism

Atheists believe there is no creator God, lesser gods or any spiritual dimension. Some believe in the basic goodness of humanity.

Some atheists are strongly against abortion, such as pro-life humanists,[4] while others have promoted mass abortion widely like Marie Stopes the eugenicist.

The number of true atheists is far less than those ticking 'no religion' in a poll. The latter may still believe and pray but not formally belong. The 2011 British census found 29,267 people declared themselves atheists out of 57 million people in the UK.

On the question 'When does life begin?' views vary. The following got high votes online, 'Life is an unbroken strand from parent to offspring. Sure, a microscopic blastocyst [human embryo] is alive, but so were the sperm and egg that it came from. There's no point at which life "began".'[5]

Some humanists use this argument to oppose abortion, saying, 'Humanists have a long history of being a secular voice of social justice and we affirm the Universal Declaration of Human Rights, as granted in Article 3, should apply to even the youngest and least developed members of our species. And we refuse to discriminate against those conceived through the violence of rape.'[6]

**Utilitarianism** is defined as 'an ethical philosophy in which the happiness of the greatest number of people in the society is considered the greatest good. So an action is morally right if its consequences lead to happiness (absence of pain), and wrong if it ends in unhappiness (pain).'[7]

This philosophy often drives healthcare decisions. People in Europe and America often practice this way. In the UK most abortion requests get a 'utilitarian' management plan. 'We will do what you request if that is what you want, and you think it will make you happy.'

Happiness is often short-term such as, 'I had five likes on Facebook', or, 'This blue sky makes me happy.' This 'happiness' needs careful weighing against the evidence of longer-term reasons for *un*happiness described in this guide – pain, infertility, broken relationship, suicide, a lost next child or cerebral palsy.

Utilitarianism may promise more than it can deliver. It may leave a legacy of disappointment, buried guilt, regret and fractured friendships.

## 3. Buddhism

The legend of Buddha born around 586 BCE is the core of the religion. Buddhist sources are their sacred texts and the way to enlightenment by following the Noble Eightfold Path. A central conviction is that one should cause no harm to others. Salvation is earned by good works and meditation. Ethical conduct includes: 1. Take no life; 2. Abstain from sexual misconduct.[8]

Buddhists regard human life as beginning at conception. For this reason, many are opposed to abortion and the Morning After Pill. In everyday practice, Buddhists, like those of other faiths, show wide variation in where they draw the line on decisions for an unwanted pregnancy.

'Japanese Buddhist tradition includes the *mizuko kuyo* ritual for post pregnancy loss, which requires a full apology from the parents to make amends to an aborted child.'[9]

---

'Abortion, from a Buddhist viewpoint, is an act of killing and is negative, generally speaking. But it depends on the circumstances. If the unborn child will be retarded or if the birth will create serious problems for the parent, these are cases where there can be an exception. I think abortion should be approved or disapproved according to each circumstance.'

Dalai Lama, *New York Times*, 28 November1993[10]

---

'Buddhists face a difficulty where an abortion is medically necessary to save the life of the mother. In such cases the moral status of an abortion will depend on the intentions of those carrying it out.'[11]

We were not able to find offers of face-to-face pregnancy counselling by Buddhists, but more general counselling can be found online.

## 4. Christianity

Christians believe in one Creator God. Their authorities are the Holy Bible and the life and teaching of Jesus Christ.

Most Christians agree the Bible puts conception as the start of an individual life, quoting passages like, 'you knit me together in my mother's womb' (Psalm 139:13) and 'from the time my mother conceived me' (Psalm 51:5).[12]

Uniquely, the Bible recounts the conception and pre-born life of Jesus and his cousin John the Baptist, all recorded by a medical doctor (Luke chapters 1 and 2).

So human life is beyond value, before and after birth, because humans, both female and male, are made in the image of God – priceless but flawed reflections of God himself.[13]

Human values like truth and love, justice and care, reflect the mother and father qualities of the God who Jesus called 'Father'.

Therefore, abortion is viewed by most Bible teachers as taking human life. The consequences are serious but have a solution: there is guilt and separation from God now, and in the next life – but God offers a way back to Him and peace with Him.

To find peace and the way back, Christians point to the world-famous story Jesus told about how God deals with broken people, and our regrets.

---

**The returning son**

'A father had two sons. The younger left home to spend his money on parties and sex. Far from home poverty strikes, so he decides to return home, face the disgrace and be a hired worker... nearing home he is amazed to see his dad running to meet him and embrace him shouting, "Let's have a big party!"'

(Paraphrase of the Prodigal Son story.)[14]

---

Christians usually support abortion if the mother's life is in danger, arguing that if nothing is done, then two lives will be lost, not one. Ectopic pregnancy is such an example since the pregnancy grows in a place where it endangers the mother from fatal bleeding.

Historically, Christians transformed Roman society by caring for unwanted newborn girls and weak babies instead of leaving them exposed outside to die. Christians opposed abortion, as did pagan doctors like famous Hippocrates 400 years before Christ.[15]

Christ's dramatic rescue of a woman caught in bed with the wrong man ignites many modern churches to welcome everyone, because Christ saved her from being stoned to death.[16]

Across the world, there are numerous centres run by Christians and others who offer pregnancy advice, medical care, counselling after pregnancy loss and practical support. See Appendix 2 'Finding Help'.

## 5. Hinduism

The guiding books are called the Vedas. For many Hindus, religion is more about what you do than what you believe. They believe in a universal God called Brahman. This God can take on many forms as gods or goddesses. Hindus believe in reincarnation – that the soul is eternal and lives many lifetimes, sometimes as a human, sometimes as an animal.

Hinduism is generally opposed to abortion, except where it is necessary to save the mother's life. Hindus believe in the principle of 'ahimsa' (non-violence), choosing the action that will do least harm to all involved. In practice, however, abortion is practiced in Hindu culture in India, because the religious ban on abortion is overruled by the cultural preference for sons. This can lead to abortion to prevent the birth of girl babies, which is called female fetocide.[17]

Hindu pregnancy and abortion counselling seems hard to find in the UK.

## 6. Islam

In Islam, the Holy Qur'an and the teaching of the prophet Mohammed are the main source of authority for worship and living. 'Whoever saves a life, has saved all mankind...' (Holy Qur'an chapter 5, verse 32).

Muslims believe in one God called Allah. His commands are to be obeyed in all matters of life. The final future of the human is weighed at the Judgement on a balance of right and wrong acts performed in their earthly life.

Talking to Muslim doctors throughout my career, all have put conception as the beginning of the individual. Marriage and family form the basic social unit of Islamic society.[18]

Secrecy and fear of family backlash may put a pregnant woman or teenager in a difficult, even a dangerous place, especially if conceived outside marriage. Strong codes of professional confidentiality should ensure the safety of those who seek advice.

---

**Shaleena says**

'Religiously I am a Muslim. For us, abortion is an unforgivable sin. Now I am excluded from salvation.'[19]

---

Shaleena's convictions and feelings after what she has gone through are common in my experience. According to online research, Islam regards abortion as wrong and *haram* (forbidden). However, all schools of Muslim law accept that abortion is permitted if continuing the pregnancy would put the mother's life in real danger. [20, 21]

Specifically, Muslim crisis pregnancy and post-abortion counselling is not easily found in the UK, although thousands of Muslims work as health professionals here and will understand the Muslim worldview.

## 7. Judaism

The Jews also have a saying, 'The one who saves a life saves the world.' They have defended the unborn since ancient times, while prioritising the mother's life over the child.

Their holy book is the Tanakh, the Old Testament of the Christian Bible. They believe in one God and that the eternal future of each person is weighed at the Judgement before God on the balance of right and wrong done in this life.

Jewish doctor Stuart Gordon, MD finds, 'Abortion is so explosive among us that we are more likely to discuss a two-state solution for Israel than dare to touch on abortion.'[22]

In 2015, the *Jewish Journal* reported that roughly half of American Jews, whether Liberal or Orthodox, say abortion should be permissible in all cases.

However, rabbis quote the Tanakh, 'God created humans in his own image... male and female he created them.'[23] Soon the Bible reports, 'Cain murdered his brother Abel, God said, "Your brother's blood cries out to me... you are under a curse."'[24]

Lord Jonathan Sacks concludes a lifetime of study with, 'Judaism is a sustained critique of power... It is about how to construct a society that honours the human person as the image and likeness of God.'[25]

**What do the prophets say?** 'Before I formed you in the womb I knew you...'[26] Isaiah says, 'The LORD called me when I was in the womb; before my birth He had pronounced my name.'[27]

There is hope in Judaism for anyone feeling cursed. The Jewish Bible has King David saying, 'God save me from blood guilt...' (the fetus has blood from the fifth week of life). 'A broken and a contrite heart oh God, you will not despise.'[28] In fact, a Jew, Jesus of Nazareth, taught that David's plea for mercy led to eternal life for David.[29]

Jewish and Messianic Jewish counselling and practical help can be found in Appendix 2 'Finding Help'.

## 8. Sikhism

Sikhs believe there is one God who is present in all things and every person; they support the equality of all men and women. Sikhs regard life as starting at conception and many do not believe that an abortion to suit a lifestyle's wishes is justified.

The Sikh sacred text, the Guru Granth Sahib, says that the body is just clothing for the soul and is discarded at death. Death leads to reincarnation as a human or an animal. On the next life, if you treat everyone with utmost respect, perhaps you will be led to God during your human incarnation.

## 9. To make mistakes is to be human

So, it appears that most of the world's faiths, and many atheists, value unborn human life highly. What do they offer people sensing they have made mistakes?

Religions vary widely over what happens to those who have regrets. Can guilt be removed? Can mental peace return?

Yes, there is a way. The old ladies Margaret and Iris (see page 121) visibly relaxed when they heard, 'Yes,' in answer to their question, 'Can God forgive me for the abortion?' and sighed with relief.

You can search many faiths. As far as we can discover, Jesus Christ alone offers the sure promise: God welcomes back all who come to Him with genuine regret.[30] He also said, 'Whoever comes to me I will never drive away.'[31]

Countless people say their regrets, shame and anxiety were wiped clean by a prayer to Jesus Christ who gave them a fresh start and a hope beyond this life. He promised a dying criminal who begged for help, 'Today you will be with me in paradise.'[32]

# Appendix 2
# Finding Help

## Introduction

Worried pregnant women and professionals can be glad that women who receive support are more likely to continue the pregnancy,[1] and enjoy positive feelings on the pregnancy after birth.[2]

Scan these pages to find which ones fit your needs. Many charities offer practical help with pregnancy, baby care, housing and finance.

These sites overlap in help offered and begin with the UK first, but many can be reached from other countries by phone or Internet.

Online counselling is more private, but phone calls and face-to-face encounters have value.

These sites begin with the UK and USA first but many are not yet inspected. Your abortion experience and outcomes are affected greatly by staff quality and a surgeon's experience.

---

**This guide is not liable for the contents of any external Internet sites listed, nor does it endorse any commercial product or service mentioned or advised on any of the sites.**

---

### Help covered here

1. General help
2. Mental health support and counselling
3. Parenting advice
4. Adoption
5. Finances and housing
6. Stories of people's pregnancy experience
7. Disability in the fetus and screening antenatally
8. Faith-based help

9. Post-abortion help
10. Global sources of help before and after the end of pregnancy
11. Help for men

## 1. General help

*Advice, helplines, blogs and information are widely available in towns across the UK and North America.*

- **Pregnancy Choices Directory**

  Gives centres of advice and counselling across the UK near you. This site also offers free pregnancy tests.

  www.pregnancychoicesdirectory.com

- **The Mix – essential support for under 25s**

  A UK-based charity providing free, confidential support for young people under 25. It offers help via helpline, email, crisis text messenger, live messenger, telephone counselling, a group chat with other young people and articles relating to pregnancy.

  www.themix.org.uk/get-support/speak-to-our-team

- **Relate – help for children and young people**

  Relate specialise in relationships so focus on advice on how to deal with pregnancy and the relationship with the father. They also run counselling sessions at centres across the UK, your nearest centre is on the 'find your nearest Relate' section.

  www.relate.org.uk/relationship-help/help-children-and-young-people/children-and-young-peoples-counselling

- **NHS Choices**

  The NHS Choices site provides a guide which talks you through your options and the process of pregnancy, birth, parenting and what support is available to you.

  www.nhs.uk/conditions/pregnancy-and-baby/teenager-pregnant/

- **Your GP, family planning clinic and school nurse**

  These people are there for you and can offer support and advice. Be aware, though, they may try to hurry you down certain routes, regardless of whether you have thought over your choice properly or not.

  www.nhs.uk/service-search/Family-planning/LocationSearch/1863

- **Image – pregnancy counselling**

  Image is a Manchester-based charity providing a compassionate response to those considering abortion and after abortion, miscarriage, stillbirth, sudden infant death or child separation.

  www.imagenet.org.uk/

- **Care in Crisis (Northern Ireland)**

  'If you want to talk to us about anything or to make a referral for counselling please contact us on **(028) 3832 9900**. Alternatively, you can **text us on 075 9433 1387** or email us at office@careincrisis.org.uk giving your name and a contact telephone number and we will call you back.'

  www.careincrisis.org.uk/

- **Gingerbread – for single parents**

  They have A-Z factsheets on debt, support available and how to look after your emotional health. They also have advice for under 18s that helps you know what you are entitled to, how you can return to education and what your future may look like. Here you can also find stories of other single parents' experiences.

  www.gingerbread.org.uk/information/young-single-parents/#

- **Family Lives**

  Family Lives aim to transform the lives of families and support parents. They have a large advice section helping you with pregnancy, bonding, sleep, feeding and a guide for dads-to-be. They also have a helpline, advice videos, forums and online parenting courses.

  www.familylives.org.uk/advice/your-family/parenting/where-can-young-parents-go-for-support/

- **Pregnancy Matters – long-established crisis pregnancy help**

  They offer counselling, housing and baby clothes, homeless help, before and after abortion counselling or lost pregnancy support. www.lifecharity.org.uk

- **Rape counselling and support will be offered by many sites in this appendix**

  https://rapecrisis.org.uk/

  https://www.nhs.uk/live-well/sexual-health/help-after-rape-and-sexual-assault/

## 2. Mental health support and counselling

*Helplines, links and advice to ensure you keep on top of your mental health.*

> **If you are having suicidal thoughts, please tell someone you trust now or call 111 in the UK.**

- **111 – The NHS doorway to urgent psychiatric help**

  When you suffer the loss of something close to you the shock and grief can feel overwhelming. With the emotional effects an abortion can bring, it's important to share your feelings with someone you can trust. You can talk it over with your family, your partner, a family doctor, a local pastor or another woman who has been through a loss.

- **Rachel's Vineyard**

  Rachel's Vineyard has centres in European countries, UK and the USA. They run healing weekends that can help you recover from the trauma abortion can bring. The weekends offer a supportive, confidential and non-judgemental atmosphere allowing you the space to deal with emotions. The weekend costs £180 but financial support is available if needed.

  http://www.rachelsvineyard.org.uk/home

- **We Are Open**

  We Are Open is an abortion recovery course run by experienced Christian professionals. They run healing weekends and provide other resources for individuals and gives guidance to churches in the UK wanting more information on post-abortion care.

  http://www.weareopen.org.uk

- **Image**

  A pregnancy support helpline that offers support both before and after an abortion. Image also has a service providing baby clothes and equipment from their Manchester office.

  http://pregnancyhelpline.co.uk

- **Cruse Bereavement Care**

  Advice and tips on grief after bereavement. It also has a helpline staffed by trained volunteers who can offer emotional support to anyone affected by bereavement. They have a list of all the Cruse areas and branches.

  https://www.cruse.org.uk

- **Mind**

  This mental health charity provides advice and support to anyone experiencing mental health problems. You can call their Infoline for confidential help or contact a local Mind centre for crisis care and housing support.

  https://www.mind.org.uk

- **The Mental Health Foundation**

  This website has an A-Z guide, podcasts and videos whilst also offering practical advice to help you and your mental health. They have a list of links they recommend to get help and support.

  https://www.mentalhealth.org.uk/your-mental-health/getting-help

- **Counselling Directory**

  A comprehensive database of UK counsellors and psychotherapists along with their training, experiences and fees. The site also has information and advice on a range of topics including abortion, bereavement, pregnancy and adoption.

  https://www.counselling-directory.org.uk

## 3. Parenting advice

*Guidance, answers and information on your parenting journey.*

- **Mumsnet**

  This site is full of advice for mums. If you are struggling with things and need help or are just looking for a bit of information and support – this is a great website full of articles and forums,

  www.mumsnet.com/Talk/active-conversations

- **Little Lullaby**

  Little Lullaby is an online community created to support young parents and young parents-to-be. You can join groups to talk about different topics with other people just like you. There is advice on things such as housing support, childcare, what to do if your baby is disabled.

  https://littlelullaby.org.uk/support-advice/

- **In the UK it is** usually possible to continue with your education while pregnant. If you are under 16, the local authority has a legal requirement to provide you with education. How this happens varies across regions and schools.

  https://www.babycentre.co.uk/x1043670/im-school-age-and-pregnant-can-i-keep-my-education-going

- **Students can visit:** www.nhs.uk/conditions/pregnancy-and-baby/maternity-paternity-leave-benefits/ This page lists the benefits you're entitled to when you're pregnant, and has information on maternity, paternity and shared parental leave.

## 4. Adoption

*Agencies, support and links to local services.*

- **Coram**

  This UK children's charity has over 40 years of experience in finding families who provide homes for life for children. Coram is one of the largest agencies in the UK. Their website explains the adoption process.

  https://www.coramadoption.org.uk/about-adoption

- **Adoption Matters**

  For over 70 years, Adoption Matters have been helping children find their future. The website has an 11-step guide to how a family will be chosen for your baby, adoption stories and a FAQ section.

  https://www.adoptionmatters.org/adoption/#our-adopters-stories

- **Adoption Support In Society Today**

  ASIST started in Somerset in 1993 as a support group for families who had adopted children. They support children, birth parents and adoptive parents. ASIST runs a national helpline so you can call, in confidence, to know more about the adoption option without committing you to anything. They are not involved in the adoption process but want to help you come to an informed decision. ASIST also signpost you to appropriate voluntary or professional organisations in your area for you to get practical help.

  http://www.babyadoptionasist.co.uk

- **Social services**

  You can contact any social services department within your local authority; they can provide help and information on adoption.

  https://www.gov.uk/find-local-council

- **Adoption UK**

  This is a government site that outlines the adoption and fostering process, birth parents' rights and fathers' rights. They also provide links to other useful sites.

  https://www.adoptionuk.org

- **Government child adoption site**

  This government site gives all the information on adoption from the early stages, through the process and how the adopting parents are picked.

  https://www.gov.uk/child-adoption

## 5. Finances and housing

*Information on what help and support is available to you and your baby.*

- **Debt IVA**

  They can help you with debts over £5,000.

  https://www.debtiva.co.uk

- **National Debt Help**

  Help with writing off unaffordable debt.

  https://www.national-debt-help.com

- **Government Care to Learn (UK ONLY)**

  The government run this to help under 20s with childcare costs while they study. It talks through who can claim, what you will get and how you do it.

  https://www.gov.uk/care-to-learn

- **CAP – for debt and poverty issues**

  Centres in major cities. To find one, open this and put your UK post code in https://capuk.org/i-want-help

- **Shelter**

  This charity helps people struggling to find housing. They offer online advice, face-to-face support, legal support and a national helpline.

  https://england.shelter.org.uk/housing_advice

## 6. Stories of people's pregnancy experience

*Reading other people's stories and how they coped can help free you from feeling isolated and feeling down. Perhaps even sharing your own story could help bring your feelings out as a step on the journey or healing. Begin reading at* https://www.pregnancychoicesdirectory.com/peoplesstories

## 7. Disability in the fetus and screening antenatally

*Finding that there is an issue with your pregnancy can be hard, so looking at these sites could provide you with some help.*

- **Antenatal Results and Choices (ARC)**

  ARC offers emotional support and non-directive counselling for people facing pain after hard pregnancy choices and they provide a range of resources and information. They also have a helpline, ARC forum and a section explaining your screening results.

  https://www.arc-uk.org

- **A Heart-breaking Choice**

  This site is 'lovingly dedicated to all who have made a heart-breaking choice'. It covers major and minor fetus problems. There are sections for spirituality, explaining diagnosis and stories of people coping with disability.

  http://www.aheartbreakingchoice.com/Default.aspx

- **Your GP and local medical services**

  GPs can help talk you through the outcome of results, scans and how sure a diagnosis is. They can provide further information to help you decide what to do.

## 8. Faith-based help

*Some pregnancy counselling services have no faith bias and others are run by a certain faith.*

- **CHRISTIANITY – Rachel's Vineyard**

  Rachel's Vineyard UK and Ireland is a safe place to renew and rebuild your life after abortion. The healing weekends offer a supportive, confidential and non-judgemental environment where women and men can deal with painful post-abortion emotions.

  http://www.rachelsvineyard.org.uk/contact-us

  http://www.rachelsvineyard.ie/

- **CHRISTIANITY – United Christian Broadcasters**

  UCB has a prayer line that offers a trained and confidential talk and prayer with a Christian for anyone, regardless of religion. You do not need to have a faith.

  https://www.ucb.co.uk/pray

- **CHRISTIANITY – The Post-abortion Healing Course**

  This course is a 9-week programme for Christians or anyone struggling after abortion loss. Visit the website for more details and your nearest course.

  https://postabortionhealingcourse.com/40/Welcome-to-the-Post-Abortion-Healing-Course

- **CHRISTIANITY – Priests for Life**

  Many resources for men and women.

  https://www.priestsforlife.org/afterabortion/index.htm

- **The Jewish Pro-Life Foundation**

  Contact to talk personally about your situation. Email Cecily at jewishpostabortionhelp@gmail.com or call 412-758-3269.[3]

- **Jewish Pregnancy Help – In Shifra's Arms**

  Jewish support for the pregnant woman. Tel. 1-888-360-5872. Text our counsellor on call: 646-632-8547

  https://jewishpregnancyhelp.org/

- **JUDAISM – Raphael Counselling Service**

  Raphael provides face-to-face counselling to those living in London, the Home Counties and the Redbridge area. The counsellors are Jewish and understand well the concerns of Jewish people. However, they can also offer the service to people who are not Jewish.

  https://www.raphaeljewishcounselling.org/whatwedo.htm

- **JUDAISM – Jewish Bereavement Counselling Service**

  A counselling website specifically for Jews. All counsellors know how deal with problems within a Jewish context.

  http://jbcs.org.uk

- **ISLAM – Muslim Women's Network**

  This site gives information of different pregnancy topics and talks you through them from a Muslim perspective. They have a helpline to talk through your issues and a text line where you can confidentially discuss your situation. They link to many other charities and support networks.

  http://www.mwnhelpline.co.uk/issuesdetail.php?id=41

- **ALL FAITHS or none – in your local area**

  Call your local church minister, Imam or other spiritual helper or helpline by searching under 'local churches, mosques and places of worship'.

## 9. Post-abortion help

*An abortion can bring many emotions and unfamiliar feelings so finding the right help can reduce any negative feelings.*

- **Freedom in Christ**

  If you still feel imprisoned by regrets, think of joining a small group on the award-winning Freedom in Christ course.

  http://www.ficm.org.uk/fic-course

- **After Abortion – the Elliot Institute**

  Dr David Reardon and others publish abortion research, educational materials and works as an advocate for women and men seeking post-abortion healing. https://www.afterabortion.org/elliot.html

## 10. Global sources of help before and after the end of pregnancy

*Many cities around the world have advice and help centres easily found on the Internet.*

**Canada**

- **Pregnancy Care Centre**

  This site goes through some questions you may have and answers them. They have local support groups in Toronto, online stories and a helpline.

  https://iamnotalone.ca/contact-us/

- **Canadian Association of Pregnancy Support Services**

  CAPSS help you find a local support centre, provide online chats and a helpline.

  https://capss.com/help/

- Youth for Christ

  Here is a list of help centres and teen-parent programmes across Canada.

  https://yfccanada.org/yfc-teen-parents-programs-in-canada-p6.php

- **Silent No More and Men and Abortion**

  https://www.silentnomoreawareness.org/shockwaves/june/men-hurting.aspx

  https://www.menandabortion.net/

**USA**

- **American Pregnancy**

  This website talks you through the choices available to you and has articles giving a wide range of information.

  https://americanpregnancy.org/unplanned-pregnancy/pregnant-teen/

- **OptionLine – 24/7 Pregnancy Help Connection**

  www.optioline.org

  Phone 800-712-HELP

- **My Choices**

  Pregnancy medical resources, Pacific Southwest. http://mychoices.org/

- **After Abortion**

  This site has tips and resources for post-abortion help. They also offer telephone and email advice both pre- and post-abortion.

  https://www.choicescommunity.co.uk/help-1/

- **Love to Know**

  This article gives you advice on what *financial help* is available to you and how you can find it. It talks you through 13 different options and gives links for you to access them.

  https://pregnancy.lovetoknow.com/financial-help-pregnant-women

- **Love to Know**

  This article goes through different sections regarding *pregnancy, abortion and support*. It gives links to different sites that can help you find the information that you need.

  https://pregnancy.lovetoknow.com/wiki/Resources_for_Pregnant_Teens

- **OPTION Adoption**

  Phone 980-224-2378

  Option-adoption.com

**India**

- www.lifeforall.org

**South Africa**

- **Choma**

  This link gives suggestions of many places you can find support, parent groups and helplines.

  https://choma.co.za/articles/78/finding-support-as-a-teen-mom#

  Amato Pregnancy Counselling Centre

  This Christian-based organisation goes through and answers questions, offers free pregnancy tests and has post-abortion support. They also offer online counselling.

  http://amato.co.za/about.html#aboutus

**New Zealand**

- **Ministry of Health**

  This site gives you signposts as to where you can find help and support through helpful subheadings.

  https://www.health.govt.nz/your-health/pregnancy-and-kids/services-and-support-during-pregnancy/support-young-pregnant-women

# Finding Help

- **Thrive Teen Parent Support Trust**

  Thrive provides workshops, training and programmes for young people and parents. They also run parent support groups and a social support service.

  http://www.thrive.org.nz

- **Kiwi Families for Passionate Parents**

  This website gives information and links to many support services and websites for teen parents in New Zealand.

  https://www.kiwifamilies.co.nz/articles/support-for-teen-parents/

- **The House of Grace**

  The house of grace offers a home for pregnant teens. There is an application form online along with information on having a baby.

  https://www.thehouseofgrace.org.nz

**Australia**

- **Kids Helpline**

  Kids Helpline provides information on what to do if you find yourself pregnant, what to do next and a helpline so you can talk things through.

  https://kidshelpline.com.au/teens/issues/could-i-be-pregnant

- **Brave Foundation**

  Here you can find answers to lots of questions, like what a pregnancy test is and what to do next. It gives further additional resources to help you in your journey.

  http://bravefoundation.org.au/support/for-girls/

- **Young Pregnant and Parenting Network**

  This site provides a list of schools that cater for pregnant and parenting young people. They also have playgroups, helplines and other types of support.

  http://youngpregnantandparenting.org.au/

- **Pregnancy help Australia**

  Find your nearest pregnancy support centre:

  https://www.pregnancysupport.com.au/resources/after-abortion-support/

**Israel and Palestine**

- **Israel – CRIB**

  'EFRAT aims to empower women to make an informed choice about the future of their pregnancy.' Counselling, practical help. Tel. 02-5454500.

  www.efrat.org.il/

- **Beadchaim**

  Pregnancy counselling and practical help for mums and their babies (providing clothing and baby items for a year). They also have a garden of life to provide a place of healing for those who have lost a child. Baedchaim have support groups to help those struggling post-abortion.

  https://www.beadchaim.com/our-services/

**Singapore**

- **Babes**

  This site gives support to teenagers who are pregnant; they have a 24-hour helpline to give you help and advice. Once you have spoken to someone they may offer you a caseworker to help you feel supported through your pregnancy.

  http://babes.org.sg/

# 11. Help for men

- **Brook UK**

  Brook has information on your rights as a dad and some explanations to situations you may find yourself in.

  https://www.brook.org.uk/your-life/advice-for-men

- **NHS Baby Guide**

  This guide talks you through the steps of pregnancy and how you can best support your partner. It also talks you through money problems, how to prepare for the birth and what to do once mum and baby are home.

  https://www.nhs.uk/conditions/pregnancy-and-baby/dad-to-be-pregnant-partner/

- **DAD info**

  This site is full of articles to help you through this journey. They also have forums and blogs to help you get support from other fathers.

  https://www.dad.info

- **Reflect**

  Reflect have support centres in North Yorkshire for men where you can go with any questions you have to get advice and help either regarding pregnancy or post-abortion.

  https://reflectyork.co.uk/what-we-do/help-for-men

# Glossary

**Abortion:** the intentional ending of a pregnancy, any time between conception and 40 weeks gestation, with the death of the unborn so they are not born alive.

**Amniotic fluid:** the watery liquid that the fetus lives in within the womb. 'My waters broke...' means when the amniotic fluid flows out through the woman's vagina before birth or during abortion.

**Anaesthetic:** medicines or injections to make you numb or sleepy so that painful procedures or surgery can be done. 'Local anaesthetic' is often used for abortion by several injections around the cervix inside the vagina. It is uncomfortable and often fails to stop severe pain.

**Antenatal care:** the care of a woman and her fetus up to and after birth.

**Anxiety:** an unpleasant sense of fear that something is threatening you. It is often linked with depression and low mood.

**Bereavement, grieving:** feeling sorrowful and mourning the death and loss of someone near to you.

**Care Quality Commission (CQC)** in the UK independently examines abortion clinics for quality and gives star ratings. They inspect and seize evidence.[1] Reports on specific clinics can be found on their website.[2] Take note that 'Safe' on a report does NOT take account of threats to individual health that any abortion brings as explained in this guide.

**Cervix:** a tightly closed muscle around the small hole at the top of the vagina. It is the gateway to the womb for the man's sperm to reach the egg. It's the outlet for the baby to be born through, or for the aborted fetus to be removed through.

**Cervical incompetence:** when the cervix is weakened, so that it cannot keep the fetus securely in the womb. One cause of this can be stretching and tearing at surgical abortion.

**Conception:** is considered the biological beginning of a human. See more in Fertilisation.

**Conscience:** a person's inner sense of right and wrong which can guide choices and actions.

**Conscientious objection:** the right of an individual to do or not to do something because of their inner convictions about what is right or wrong, good or harmful. This can apply to them or their action for someone else.

The UK Abortion Act upholds the rights of healthcare staff to have conscientious objection against taking part in abortion while upholding a woman's right to another clinical opinion.

**Consent:** when a patient gives permission to someone else to interfere with their body by a medical procedure. In abortion European (EU), Canadian and Australian law specify *full information* with understanding of unintended side-effects – even if rare – must be made clear.

**Contraception:** attempts to prevent pregnancy by natural or artificial means like the Pill, coil, and barriers such as condoms; it may include methods that destroy young embryos in early pregnancy, which some argue is abortion.

**Contractions:** the periodic tightening and relaxing of the womb which can feel like cramping around the back or abdomen.

**Counsellor:** a professional who sees a person privately to help them explore what is best for them according to their circumstances, feelings and conscience.

**CVS (Chorionic Villus Sampling):** commonly known as 'amniocentesis'. This involves a needle going through the mother's tummy or the vagina into the placenta to try and extract some blood from the fetus to look at the genes. The side-effect risk of losing the fetus happens at 1 in 50 procedures.

**Depression:** a feeling and illness like heaviness, darkness and loss of hope which affects your ability to live properly and often comes with anxiety as well. Lost hope after abortion can provoke sudden severe depression and suicide.

**Disenfranchised grief:** the grief of bereavement which cannot be shown easily to friends, family or in public because of the feeling that one is ashamed or 'not meant to be grieving'. Abortion can provoke disenfranchised grief, because abortion is usually done in the belief it should solve a problem not create a new problem like major loss.

**Ectopic pregnancy:** when a young human embryo is not growing in the womb, but somewhere else. This brings the risk of bursting and bleeding internally.

**EDD: Expected Date of Delivery** of the baby which is calculated from the first day of the last menstrual period or a dating ultrasound scan.

**Embryo:** a human being from their conception onwards and up to eight weeks of pregnancy age, at which point they are known as a fetus or baby till birth.

**Ethical:** something that is morally right. Unethical means it is morally wrong.

**Fallopian tube:** shown in the picture on page 54, it is the short pipe in the woman, two or three centimetres long, which opens into the top of the womb on both sides. The other end has tentacles which capture the freshly produced egg from the woman's ovary. Tiny hairs waft the egg along the tube towards the womb. In the tube the egg meets the man's sperm swimming up from the womb and often fertilisation happens – a unique new embryo begins.

**Fertilisation:** (also called conception) is the mysterious mixing of an egg and sperm to start a new human being – an embryo. It's the biological uniting of the genes of two people to become an individual of the next generation. Within an hour this embryo sends a hormone signal to the mother that pregnancy has begun.

**Fetal abnormality and disability:** when there is a minor or major physical or genetic disease discovered in the fetus.

**Fetus:** the medical name for the unborn baby in the womb from the 8th week of pregnancy until birth.

**FFTP:** means a woman's First Full-Term Pregnancy where the baby is born older than 38 weeks in the mother.

**General anaesthetic:** the procedure to put you into a deep sleep using powerful medicines so that painful procedures can be done.

**Gestational age:** the duration of the pregnancy, which is also the age of the fetus in weeks from either conception or the last menstrual period (LMP). Using the LMP, normal pregnancy is 40 weeks, or between 38–42 weeks. Preterm birth is 37 weeks or younger.

**Haemorrhage:** severe bleeding that can threaten life and may need blood transfusion. Possible causes for the purposes of this book include all types of abortion, infection after abortion and childbirth.

**Heart area:** anything that reflects someone's deeply held values.

**HCG (Human Chorionic Gonadotropin)** is the hormone signal detected by the positive pregnancy test. It is sent out by the embryo to the mother within hours of conception.

**Implantation:** is the burrowing of the week-old embryo into the soft lining of the woman's womb. Blood vessels form and reach out to unite mother and embryo as the placenta. Nutrients and oxygen are passed from the woman to the embryo.

**Infertility:** when a couple or a woman cannot conceive a baby (subfecundity) after one year of regular sex without contraception or bring a pregnancy to a successful live birth. This guide explains several reasons why failure to deliver a healthy baby is linked to prior abortion.

**Labour:** the woman's process of delivering her fetus at a birth (or it can be at an abortion).

**LMP:** the date of the first day of the woman's Last Menstrual Period. This is useful for calculating the age of the pregnancy. The embryo is about two weeks younger than the time back to when the LMP happened. So, on the date of the first missed period after the LMP the embryo is about two weeks old. Websites like https://www.babycentre.co.uk/a549805/how-to-count-your-pregnancy-in-weeks-and-months help you calculate your dates.

**Local anaesthetic:** a medicine usually given by injection to numb part of the body to pain.

**Mammogram:** a special x-ray of the breast which can detect early breast cancer.

**Medical abortion:** abortion induced by hormones and chemicals given by mouth, in the vagina or through a vein. Also called 'Pill Abortion'.

# Glossary

**Menstrual cycle:** the woman's natural process of monthly bleeding when not pregnant. It is preparing your body for pregnancy each month.

**Microcephalic:** a fetus, baby or adult with an unusually small head.

**Midwife:** a specialist to help women through pregnancy, birth and recovery from birth. Most midwives have resisted involvement in abortion.

**Miscarriage:** the spontaneous loss of a fetus which is too young to survive outside the womb.

**Moral:** behaviour and choices which are ethically correct according to one's inner convictions or the teaching of religious leaders.

**NHS:** The National Health Service of Great Britain.

**NIPT:** means Non-Invasive Prenatal Testing.

**Oestrogen (Estrogen in US):** a female hormone released in large amounts throughout pregnancy. In a first pregnancy, it changes breast tissue from a cancer-safer state before conception to a cancer-risky state in early pregnancy. This change is permanent unless the pregnancy continues to 32 weeks – at this point on the breasts become more cancer resistant for life.

**Ovulation:** the monthly release of an ovum from a woman's ovary.

**Ovum:** a woman's egg cell, the size of a dot, which can unite with a man's sperm cell at conception to begin a new human. A teenager or woman of reproductive age ovulates each month before her period.

**PID (Pelvic Inflammatory Disease):** a persisting and painful illness of the pelvis following infection, commonly due to chlamydia now.

**Placenta (Afterbirth):** the pad of tissues and blood vessels that join the woman to her embryo, later fetus. It collects the mother's food and oxygen for the baby. It grows on a stalk (the umbilical cord) connected to the mother's womb. The placenta also expels waste from the baby to the mother. Following birth the placenta is normally delivered through the vagina – hence it's called the 'afterbirth'.

**Placenta Praevia:** is an abnormal position of the placenta where it lies too low in the uterus. If it covers the cervix (the exit hole in the uterus) the placenta can bleed through the vagina endangering the woman and baby.

**Pregnancy:** a word that is often used, as in this guide, to mean the unborn embryo/fetus/baby and placenta. For instance, 'She ended the pregnancy,' is another way of saying she had an abortion. 'Pregnancy' is also used to mean, 'Being pregnant; the period from conception to birth when a woman carries a developing fetus in her uterus.'[3]

**Prem:** short for **'premature birth'** or **'preterm birth'** where birth happened at gestational age less than 37 weeks.

**Preterm labour:** is when the woman's uterus begins contracting too soon which threatens to cause premature birth unless it can be stopped.

**RCOG:** is the Royal College of Obstetricians and Gynaecologists, based in London, UK. They advise the British government on abortion law, train all OBGYNs, train and license abortion doctors and oversee the abortion service standards. See also the Care Quality Commission (CQC) above.

**Screening:** testing people to see if there is a disease present. This includes breast cancer screening for older women and screening tests in pregnancy on the mother and fetus.

**Sepsis:** overwhelming infection which threatens life.

**STIs:** are Sexually Transmitted Infections such as Chlamydia, Gonorrhoea and HIV-AIDS among 30 or more others.

**Surgical abortion:** ending the pregnancy by inserting a large suction tube through the vagina into the womb and sucking out the fetus and placenta – rather than using drugs and chemicals – or scraping out the womb or surgical destruction and removal of the fetus.

**Ultrasound scan:** a painless and harmless way of looking at the fetus from very early pregnancy until birth.

**Umbilical cord:** is the tube of blood vessels connecting the fetus to the woman. The placenta is at the other end from the fetus and is implanted in the womb.

**Uterus:** is the womb.

**Womb:** the reproductive organ in the woman's pelvis, the shape and size of a pear in the non-pregnant woman. It is where fetuses grow until birth.

# Acknowledgements

First, thanks go to my patients who trusted me with your lives and secrets for over 40 years. I can't name you, but I appreciate you. Names and details have been changed to protect identities.

It's been a female-driven team effort. If you have read this far you will see what a complex subject it is! As with the first edition, *Pregnancy and Abortion: Your Choice*, only a team of co-writers and researchers – some world-class experts – could make it possible. Thank you and my wonderful wife and kids on this journey. Special thanks to Dr Esther Lüthy, tireless co-writer and critic, and Christine Fidler making time in a busy schedule.

Thanks again to specialists in UK, Canada, South America, Israel, Australia, India and Africa. Prof. John Wyatt updated the 'Premature Birth' chapter with Margaret Eames (FSS, FRSPH, MSc, DLSHTM, PGCE, BSc) and Dr Greg Gardner.

Joel Brind PhD, P. Carroll statistician, Brent Rooney, K. Neeley, Brigid Houghton and my late cousin Benjamin Houghton – thank you. Dr R. Dixon PhD medical statistician – everyone on such a task needs a Bob – diligent, friendly and instantly available for months.

James Evans kindly researched fetal pain feelings and supplied the table of milestones in chapter 8 'Feelings of a Fetus'.

Among teens and twenties Isabel, Caitlin, Celia, Dan, Fiona, Jess Wood, and Ruth Smith with your talents.

Once again, Malcolm and Sarah from Malcolm Down and Sarah Grace Publishing have been patient, steady hands steering this project with their expert copy-editors Chloe Evans and Louise Stenhouse.

The 4H Tool with Head/Heart contains ideas first devised by the Firgrove Centre (now Alder Trust). Our thanks to the Alder Trust for permission to use these ideas.

*Complications: Abortion's Impact on Women*, 2013 and second edition, 2018, have been a mine of information.

Image credits: Woman in crowd, Joseph Grunenthal. Beach picture, Zac Minor. Pregnancy test, rawpixel.com / Freepik. Weighing scales, rawpixel.com / Freepik. Thank you, Dr Pierucci, for the picture of an anencephalic child in a girl's arms.

We have all dug for truth in hidden corners, but the final responsibility is mine.

# Notes

Here you can jot down thoughts, feelings and any questions you may have.

Take these to any appointment, clinic or antenatal, along with:

**My past medical history:**

* My personal doctor name, address, phone number.

* My past medical history: pregnancies, illnesses, operations, treatments, drugs and food allergies, medication, STIs, contraception, steroids, prescription medicines, supplements not prescribed by a doctor.

**My questions to ask at the clinic:**

1.

2.

3.

4.

5.

# Further Resources and Reading

It is surprisingly difficult to find balanced information on abortion decision-making. The countless general public, who really need quality information seem deafened by the noise from the pro- and anti-abortion camps.

Many of the websites mentioned in this book and the endnotes have good information – which we are not responsible for.

The investigative film *HUSH* is easy to watch with facts everyone should know – I have checked many of these with experts. Director Punam Kumar Gill (Mighty Motion Pictures/Mighty Distributors Inc., 2016).

**Further reading**

For professionals and patients, the booklet *Abortion – Doctors Duties and Rights* (London: Christian Medical Fellowship, 2016) by Philippa Taylor will inform professionals and patients about many practical aspects of where they stand in the UK law.

*Complications: Abortion's Impact on Women*, second edition, revised 2018, is a unique reference resource for professionals and policymakers.

Dr David Reardon's Elliott Institute/Afterabortion.org in Canada maintains a huge pool of research and advice for lay people and professionals,[1] as does the medical AAPLOG in the States.[2]

The Breast Cancer Prevention Institute run by American surgeons has many fact sheets, papers and simple biological explanations.[3]

# Endnotes

## A Guide for You

[1] Photo: https://unsplash.com/photos/xUnhfZNBm7s

## Chapter 1

[1] See more in NHS Choices at https://www.nhs.uk/common-health-questions/pregnancy/how-soon-can-i-do-a-pregnancy-test/(accessed 24 May 2019).

[2] See more in NHS Choices link above which also has: https://www.nhs.uk/conditions/pregnancy-and-baby/1-2-3-weeks-pregnant/(accessed 24 May 2019).

[3] *Human Reproduction*, April 2015 30(4), pp. 751–760 (accessed 24 August 2019).

[4] https://www.acog.org/Clinical-Guidance-and-Publications/Committee-Opinions/Committee-on-Gynecologic-Practice/Clinical-Challenges-of-Long-Acting-Reversible-Contraceptive-Methods (accessed 13 August 2019).

[5] 'Emergency contraception and impact on abortion rates', L. Michie MB ChB MRCOG MFSRH MD, S.T. Cameron MB ChB FRCOG MFSRH MD, 3 July 2019, https://www.sciencedirect.com/science/article/pii/S1521693419300872 (accessed 24 August 2019). Also see https://www.ncbi.nlm.nih.gov/pmc/articles/PMC4447791

## Chapter 3

[1] Further evidence of poor-quality counselling in abortion clinics in the US and UK comes from two of the most experienced American and British gynaecologists in practice in 2019 – personal communications face-to-face with Dr M. Houghton, April 2019 and May 2019 respectively. Their names can be supplied on request via the website.

## Chapter 6

[1] 'Women's Voices: narratives of the abortion experience', p. 326–371 in *Complications: Abortion's Impact on Women*, 2nd Edition (The deVeber Institute for Bioethics and Social Research, 2018).

[2] Ibid.

# Chapter 7

[1] D.T. Baird et al., *Human Reproduction*, April 2015, 30(4), pp. 751–76, https://www.ncbi.nlm.nih.gov/pmc/articles/PMC4447791/ (accessed 24 August 19).

[2] Based on the biological arguments in the article J.K. Findlay et al., 'Human embryo: a biological definition', *Human Reproduction* 22 (April 2007): pp. 905–11 found at: https://academic.oup.com/humrep/article-abstract/22/4/905/695880/Human-embryo-a-biological-definition (accessed 26 September 2017).

[3] https://www.shutterstock.com/image-vector/uterus-ovaries-organs-female-reproductive-system-37063382

[4] *The Telegraph,* 27 April 2016 http://www.telegraph.co.uk/sci-ence/2016/04/26/bright-flash-of-light-marks-incredible-moment-life-begins-when-s/

[5] Watch conception/fertilisation in one minute: https://www.youtube.com/watch?v=OD1gW88Lm-Y
Stunning three-minute video for the first 20 days of a fetus: www.babycenter.com/2_inside-pregnancy-your-baby-takes-shape_10354437.bc

[6] http://www.babymed.com/positive-pregnancy-test-how-early-after-implantation (accessed 23 February 2017).

[7] By kind permission of Professor Teresa Woodruff, Northwestern University, USA.

[8] K.E. McGrath and J. Palis, 'Hematopoiesis in the yolk sac: more than meets the eye', *Experimental Hematology* 33(9) (September 2005) https://www.ncbi.nlm.nih.gov/pu-bmed/16140150.

[9] *Planet Child* on ITV television, UK, 9.30pm, 1st May 2019.

[10] S. Sekulic, et al., 'Appearance of fetal pain could be associated with maturation of the mesodiencephalic structures', *Journal of Pain Research* 9 (November 2016), pp. 1031–8 https://www.ncbi.nlm.nih.gov/pmc/articles/PMC5115678/#!po=1.66667

[11] R.W. Loftin, et al., 'Late Preterm Birth', *Reviews in Obstetrics and Gynecology* 3(1) (Winter 2010), pp. 10–19. https://www.ncbi.nlm.nih.gov/pmc/articles/PMC2876317/

[12] www.ehd.org/see-baby-pregnancy-guide.php (accessed 24 May 2019).

[13] These are Swedish figures kindly supplied by Professor of Paediatrics, Martin McCaffrey MD, 6 April 2019 in a lecture attended by the author.

[14] *Babies: Their Wonderful World*, UK television, BBC 2, 9pm, 3 December 2018 https://www.bbcearth.com/blog/?article=are-babies-born-good-or-evil (accessed 15 August 2019).

# Chapter 8

[1] Kirti N. Saxena, 'Anaesthesia for Fetal Surgeries', *Indian Journal of Anaesthesia* 53(5) (October 2009), pp. 554–9. Found at https://www.ncbi.nlm.nih.gov/pmc/articles/ PMC2900087/ (accessed 27 May 2019).

[2] Lecture to the author, 6 April 2019, Indianapolis, USA.

[3] Foetuses: Pain, Parliamentary Written question – 204402; asked by Sir John Hayes (South Holland and The Deepings MP) 20 December 2018, answered by Jackie Doyle Price (Department of Health), 10 January 2019.

[4] Dr Byron C. Calhoun, MD, FACOG, FACS, FASAM, MBA. Personal communication, November 2018.

[5] http://www.nrlc.org/uploads/fetalpain/AnandPainReport.pdf

[6] S. Sekulic, et al., 'Appearance of fetal pain could be associated with maturation of the mesodiencephalic structures', *Journal of Pain Research* 9 (November 2016), pp. 1031–8 https://www.ncbi.nlm.nih.gov/pmc/articles/PMC5115678/#!po=1.66667

[7] https://www.washingtonpost.com/opinions/what-the-push-for-legal-until-birth-abortion-tells-us-about-the-abortion-debate/2019/02/01/7830bf94-25ac-11e9-90cd-dedb0c92dc17_story.html?noredirect=on&utm_term=.ec9278785b97 (accessed 8 July 2019).

[8] https://www.rcog.org.uk/globalassets/documents/guidelines/rcogfetalawarenesswpr0610.pdf

[9] https://www.bpas.org/abortion-care/abortion-treatments/the-abortion-pill/feticide/

[10] https://www.ncbi.nlm.nih.gov/pmc/articles/PMC4402596/

[11] Page 25 of https://www.rcog.org.uk/globalassets/documents/guidelines/rcogfetalawarenesswpr0610.pdf (accessed 8 July 2019).

[12] Lecture to the author, 6 April 2019, Indianapolis, USA.

[13] https://assets.publishing.service.gov.uk/government/uploads/system/uploads/attachment_data/file/763174/2017-abortion-statistics-for-england-and-wales-revised.pdf (accessed 8 July 2019).

[14] Personal discussion with Prof. Byron Calhoun, MD, OB/GYN, October 2018.

[15] Perinatal Hospice: Family-Centered Care of the Fetus with a Lethal Condition. Michelle D'Almeida, D.O. Roderick F. Hume, Jr, MD, Anthony Lathrop, C.N.M. Adaku Njoku, MD, Byron C. Calhoun, MD, *Journal of American Physicians and Surgeons* Volume 11 Number 2 Summer, 2006. *The Journal of Reproductive Medicine* Volume 48 Number 5, May 2003. *The Journal of Reproductive Medicine*, 'Perinatal Hospice Comprehensive Care for the Family of the Fetus with a Lethal Condition', Byron C. Calhoun, Col, MC, USAF, Peter Napolitano,

LTC,MC, USA, Melissa Terry, CAPT,MC, USA, Carie Bussey, CAPT,AN, and Nathan J. Hoeldtke, LTC,MC, USA.

[16] Photo by kind permission in April 2019 of Dr Robin Pierucci MD, Neonatologist.

[17] Sekulic's 2016 review.

[18] https://assets.publishing.service.gov.uk/government/uploads/system/uploads/attachment_data/file/763174/2017-abortionstatistics-for-england-and-wales-revised.pdf

## Chapter 9

[1] www.nhs.uk/conditions/pregnancy-and-baby/maternity-paternity-leave-benefits

[2] https://www.gov.uk/asylum-support/what-youll-get

[3] www.nhs.uk/conditions/pregnancy-and-baby/maternity-paternity-leave-benefits/

[4] https://england.shelter.org.uk/housing_advice

[5] https://lifecharity.org.uk/pregnant-nowhere-live/

[6] https://www.babycentre.co.uk/x1043670/im-school-age-and-pregnant-can-i-keep-my-education-going

[7] https://www.gov.uk/care-to-learn/what-youll-get-while-you-study

[8] https://www.nus.org.uk/en/news/information-for-student-parents/

[9] www.gingerbread.org.uk

[10] www.home-start.org.uk.

[11] https://www.family-action.org.uk/what-we-do/early-years/childrens-centres__trashed/

## Chapter 10

[1] https://www.fertilityauthority.com/articles/famous-people-who-are-adopted (accessed 14 February 2019).

[2] http://www.onetruegift.com/2018/10/adoption-and-parenting-reads-of-the-week-60/ (accessed 25 April 2019).

[3] The site http://corambaaf.org.uk/ has good information and stories.

[4] Hugh Muir, 'The Truth About Inter-racial Adoption', *The Guardian* (3 November 2010). https://www.theguardian.com/society/2010/nov/03/inter-racial-adoption (accessed 25 May 2019).

[5] Susan Rose, Founder of Fetal Alcohol Syndrome Network of New York City https://www.quora.com/profile/Susan-Rose-109 (accessed 25 May 2019).

[6] Dr Kirsty Saunders, MBChB, DCH. Adoption paediatrician in the UK.

[7] Quoted from www.option-adoption.com Tel. +980-224-2378.

[8] https://www.americanadoptions.com/pregnant/waiting_adoptive_families (accessed 26 April 2019).

[9] Creating a Family https://creatingafamily.org/adoption/comparison-country-charts/ (accessed May 2019).

[10] Dept. of Education: Children looked after in England (including adoption), year ending 31 March 2018. https://assets.publishing.service.gov.uk/government/uploads/system/uploads/attachment_data/file/664995/SFR50_2017-Children_looked_after_in_England.pdf (accessed 25 May 2019).

[11] See for instance, 'Women's Voices: narratives of the abortion experience', p. 326–371 in *Complications: Abortion's Impact on Women*, 2nd Edition (The deVeber Institute for Bioethics and Social Research, 2018). Post Traumatic Syndrome Disorder videos, OperationOutcry.org, San Antonio, Texas.

## Chapter 11

[1] 'The Care of Women Requesting Induced Abortion', RCOG (November 2011, accessed 7 June 2019). For a ballpark figure of immediate physical complications after abortion (in the first 6 weeks) 1 in 10 women is useful. This combines multiple studies from Canada, the USA and New Zealand and allows for the fact that many complications are not reported. See page 98–110 of *Complications: Abortion's Impact on Women*, 2nd Edition, 2018. The RCOG gave an immediate (first 6 weeks after abortion) physical complication rate of 11% in the year 2000 but their revised guidelines in 2011 did not report an overall rate.

[2] Ibid.

[3] 'A register-based study of 42,619 first-trimester abortions in Finland', *Complications: Abortion's Impact on Women*, 2nd Edition, (The deVeber Institute for Bioethics, 2018). Niinimaki M., Pouta, Bloigu A., et al., 'Immediate complications after medical compared with surgical termination of pregnancy', *Obstetrics and Gynaecology*, 2009, October; 114(4);795–804.

[4] Professor Byron Calhoun OBGYN, W. Virginia, November 2017. 74

[5] Des Spence, *BMJ* 2013; 346: f927 (16 February). Royal College of Surgeons, October 2016 https://www.rcseng.ac.uk/news-and-events/media-centre/press-releases/surgeons-warn-nhs-failing-to-implement-patientconsent-rules/

[6] https://www.rcog.org.uk/globalassets/documents/guidelines/abortion_guideline_summary.pdf 2011, (accessed 9 July 2019).

[7] *Complications: Abortion's Impact on Women*, 2nd Edition, pp.217–226.

[8] Grossman D., Blachard K., Blumenthal P., 'Complications after 2nd trimester surgical and medical abortion', *Reproductive Health Matters* 2008; 16 (31): 173–182. Other studies also quoted in *Complications: Abortion's Impact on Women*, 2nd Edition, p.224.

[9] Pastuuszak A.L., Schuler L., Speck-Martins C.E. et al., use of Misoprostol during pregnancy and Mobius syndrome in infants. *NEJM* 1998; 338: pp.1881–5.

[10] Kmietowicz Z., (2015) 'Medical abortions are more common than surgery for the first time in 2014 in England and Wales', *BMJ* 350:h3177.

[11] Raymond E.G., Shannon C., Weaver M.A. and Winicoff B., (2013) 'First-trimester medical abortion with Mifipristone 200 mg and Misoprostol a systematic review', *Contraception* 87:26–37.

[12] 'A comparative study of surgical and medical procedures: 932 pregnancy terminations up to 63 days gestation', *Human Reproduction* 2001; 16 (one): pp. 67–71.

[13] *Complications: Abortion's Impact on Women*, 2nd Edition, p.220.

[14] https://www.fda.gov/Drugs/DrugSafety/PostmarketDrugSafetyInformationfor PatientsandProviders/ucm492705.htm (accessed 27 February 2019).

[15] https://www.telegraph.co.uk/news/health/news/9164142/Doctors-signing-off-abortions-for-women-they-have-nevermet. html (accessed 26 August 2019).

[16] Delgado G. MD, Condly S. PhD, Davenport M. MD, MS, Tinnakornsrisuphap T. PhD., Mack J. PhD, NP, RN, Khauv J. BS, and Zhou P., 'A Case Series Detailing the Successful Reversal of the Effects of Mifepristone Using Progesterone', *Issues in Law and Medicine*, Volume 33, Number 1, 2018.

[17] www.abortionpillreversal.com, https://optionline.org/ Call 1-877-558-0333, Text 'HELPLINE' to 313131 www.heartbeatservices.org/chemical-abortion-and-reversal-how-your-center-can-help

[18] Head of the Royal College of Obstetricians and Gynaecologists https://www.theguardian.com/world/2017/oct/05/makeaccess-to-abortion-easier-uks-top-obstetrician-demands (accessed 9 September 2019).

[19] Gynaecologists in Yorkshire (UK) told us confidentially (in 2017 and 2019) their NHS hospital often receives women after poor quality private abortions. The physical details for the woman and her unborn are too distressing to write.

[20] *Complications: Abortion's Impact on Women*, 2nd Edition.

[21] Dr Anthony Levatino ob-gyn who formerly performed abortions. He testified to a Congressional subcommittee see video https://www.youtube.com/watch?v=8szDctI9lXM

[22] https://www.bpas.org/abortion-care/abortion-treatments/the-abortion-pill/

feticide/ (accessed 25 February 2019).

[23] See theabortionsurvivors.com/abortion-survivors-and-their-stories/sarah-smith/ In 2008, 66 British babies were born alive. UK Confidential Inquiry into Maternal Deaths 2008.

[24] https://aaplog.org/save-the-life-of-the-mother and https://www.feministsforlife. org/what-about-the-life-of-the-mother/ (accessed 16-11-19).

[25] As a young doctor, I had to destroy a live fetus that got blocked at birth. I was alone on a remote island without specialist training. The mother lived to care for her children.

[26] https://www.england.nhs.uk/atlas_case_study/increasing-neonatal-palliative-c (accessed 15 April 2019).

[27] https://aaplog.org/save-the-life-of-the-mother/ ).

[28] Repeated reports to the author 2010-19 in South Yorkshire, UK.

[29] A North Yorkshire UK gynaecologist speaking to the author MH, 2019.

[30] CQC report 2016, https://www.cqc.org.uk/sites/default/files/new_reports/ AAAF4825.pdf (accessed 15 April 2019).

[31] https://www.washingtonexaminer.com/planned-parenthood-lies-about-itself (accessed 15 April 2019).

[32] *Daily Telegraph* and Channel 4 TV *Dispatches*, https://www.telegraph. co.uk/science/2016/03/15/abortedbabies-incinerated-to-heat-uk-hospitals/ (accessed 15 April 2019).

[33] www.beadchaim.com, phone +972-2-624-2516.

[34] Personal conversation with a teacher in South Yorkshire 2016.

[35] 'Injury, deaths, suicides and homicides associated with pregnancy, Finland 1987–2000', Gissler M., et al., (2005), *European Journal of Public Health*, 15, pp. 459–463.

[36] https://sepsistrust.org/about/about-sepsis/ (accessed 28-11-19).

## Chapter 12

[1] ACOG (American College of OBGYN, May 1969, 'The inherent risks of a therapeutic abortion are serious and may be life threatening...'

[2] For example, in New South Wales, a former patient sued a hospital and an abortionist for failing to warn her that she might subsequently have a bad psychiatric reaction, and for failure to warn of the increased breast-cancer risk. http://www.life.org.nz/ abortion/aboutabortion/aboutabortion14/ (accessed 8 June 2019).

3. https://reproductiverights.org/worldabortionlaws?category[294]=294 (accessed 30 August 19).

4 Personal communication from a practising Irish obstetrician, May 2019.

5 https://www.bbc.co.uk/news/uk-northern-ireland-49831856 (accessed 26-11-19)

6 https://www.nationalreview.com/2017/08/forced-abortion-coerced-women-pregnancy-economic-pressure-pro-life-help/.
https://www.independent.co.uk/news/uk/home-news/pregnancy-coercion-reproduction-abortion-a8834306.html. (Accessed 23-11-19).

7 For example, 21 October 2017, https://www.independent.co.uk/news/uk/home-news/abortions-marie-stopes-clinic-bonusespersuade-women-investigation-a8012171.html

8 https://www.bbc.co.uk/news/world-us-canada-47940659 (31 May 2019).

9 Standard for Adverse Risk Warnings: US Ninth Circuit Court ruled: 'We believe a risk must be disclosed even if it is but a potential risk rather than a conclusively determined risk. It may be that these risks had not yet been documented or accepted as a fact in the medical profession. Nonetheless, under the doctrine of informed consent, these risks should have been disclosed. Medical knowledge should not be limited to what is generally accepted by the profession.' J. Kindley, 'The Fit Between the Elements for an Informed Consent Cause of Action and the Scientific Evidence Linking Induced Abortion with Breast Cancer Risk', *Wisconsin Law Review* (1998): pp. 1595–1644, http://www.kindleylaw.com/wpcontent/uploads/2009/05/1998WLR15952 pdf.

10 https://en.wikipedia.org/wiki/Abortion_in_Australia, accessed 26-11-19

11 Montgomery (appellant) v. Lanarkshire Health Board (respondent) (2015) UKSC 11, on appeal from (2013) CSHIH. Current Department of Health guidance on abortion provision stipulates that women must be given impartial, accurate and evidence-based information (verbal and written) delivered neutrally and covering alternatives to abortion. The GMC demands cooperative clinical decision making.

12 https://www.loc.gov/law/help/abortion-legislation/europe.php accessed 26-11-19

13 GMC and BMA guidance quoted in Philippa Taylor, *Abortion: Doctors' Duties and Rights*, (London: Christian Medical Fellowship, 2016), p. 43.

14 Quoted in *Abortion: Doctors' Duties and Rights*.

15 The UK's GMC has said this for years.

16 Two similar cases were reported to the authors by colleagues in the past 4 years.

17 Letter from the Right Hon. Jeremy Hunt MP, Secretary of State for Health, London, to the author, 2017.

18 https://www.independent.co.uk/news/health/selective-abortions-gender-tests-girls-uk-labour-a8540851.html

[19] https://www.unfpa.org/news/sex-selection-leads-dangerous-gender-imbalance-new-programme-tackle-root-causes

[20] https://www.comresglobal.com/wp-content/uploads/2017/05/Where-DoThey-Stand-Abortion-Survey-Data-Tables.pdf (accessed 5 August 2019).

[21] https://www.comresglobal.com/wp-content/uploads/2017/05/Where-DoThey-Stand-Abortion-Survey-Data-Tables.pdf and https://www.comresglobal. com/wp-content/uploads/2017/11/CARE_abortion-survey_October-2017_ v3.pdf (both accessed 10 June 2019).

[22] https://blogs.spectator.co.uk/2017/05/new-poll-shows-good-deal-uneasecurrent-abortion-law/ (accessed 10 July 2019).

[23] Letter from the General Medical Council to the CEO of Christian Medical Fellowship, London. (26 March 2008).

[24] This is a typical proportion based on my own questioning of trainee doctors in England over the past 15 years.

[25] Conversation with a Yorkshire specialist obstetrician and gynaecologist April 2019.

[26] A Legal Guide for Healthcare Professionals, Alliance Defending Freedom, October 2016, ADFlegal.org

[27] Information based on the CMA code of ethics, https://www.cma.ca/Assets/ assetslibrary/document/en/advocacy/policyresearch/CMA_Policy_Code_of_ ethics_of_the_Canadian_Medical_Association_Update_2004_PD04-06-e.pdf and Abortion Rights Coalition of Canada, June 2018, http://www.arcc-cdac. ca/postionpapers/95-appendixpolicies-conscientious-objection-healthcare.pdf (accessed 11th June 2019). A provincial legislation holds greater force than a professional regulatory body or the CMA, such as with Manitoba Bill 34 in 2017 which enshrined a physician's right to refuse to do assisted suicide. file:///C:/ Users/Mark/AppData/Local/Microsoft/Windows/INetCache/Content.Outlook/ FK8LRQ5T/Bill34manitoba.pdf (accessed 11 June 2019).

[28] http://www.jebmh.com/data_pdf/2_Srinivas%20Rao.pdf (accessed 10 June 2019). Srinivasa Rao Tatavarti, Vidyullatha Arimilli, 'Preterm Birth Association with Cerebral Palsy', *Journal of Evidence-based Medicine and Healthcare*; Volume 2, Issue 18, 4 May 2015; Page: 2476–2479.

## Chapter 13

[1] 'The Care of Women Requesting Induced Abortion', RCOG (November 2011) (accessed April 2019).

[2] Spitz, Irving, et al., 'Early Pregnancy Termination with Mifepristone and Misoprostol in the United States', *The New England Journal of Medicine*, 338:1241–1247 (30 April 1998) online (accessed 7 August 2017).

[3] G. Penny, 'Treatment of pain during medical abortion', *Contraception* 74(1) (July 2006), pp. 45–7.

[4] K.R. Meckstroth, K. Mishra, 'Analgesia/pain management in the first trimester surgical abortion', *Clinical Obstetrics and Gynaecology* (June 2009) 52(2): pp. 160–70.

[5] S. Suliman, et al., 'Comparison of pain, cortisol levels, and psychological distress in women undergoing surgical termination of pregnancy under local anaesthesia versus intravenous sedation', *BMC Psychiatry* 7(24) (June 2007), pp. 24–32, https://www.ncbi. nlm.nih.gov/pmc/articles/PMC1899490/

[6] 'The Care of Women Requesting Induced Abortion', RCOG (November 2011), (accessed 7 June 2019).

[7] https://sepsistrust.org/about/about-sepsis/ (accessed 28-11-19)

[8] B. Major, M. Applebaum, L. Beckman, et al., 'Report of the APA Task Force on Mental Health and Abortion', American Psychological Association (2008), http://www.apa. org/pi/women/programs/abortion/mental-health.pdf

[9] Sullins, D.P. Affective and Substance Abuse Disorders Following Abortion by Pregnancy Intention in the United States: A Longitudinal Cohort Study. *Medicina* **2019**, 55, 741 (accessed 22-11-19). 'Although some studies have found little to no psychological distress associated with abortion, **to date no study has documented mental health benefits for women from abortion.**'

[10] Creinin MD, 'Randomised comparison of efficacy, acceptability and cost of medical versus surgical abortion', *Contraception* 2000; 62 (3): 117–24, p. 117.

[11] S.G. Kaali, et al., 'The frequency and management of uterine perforations during first trimester abortions', *American Journal of Obstetrics & Gynecology* 61(2) (August 1989), pp. 406–8, www.ajog.org/article/0002-9378(89)90532-2/pdf (accessed 7 August 2017).

[12] Leibner E.C., 'Delayed presentation of uterine perforation', *Annals of Emergency Medicine* 1995 November; 26(5):643–6, p.643. From p. 190, *Complications: Abortion's Impact on Women*, 2nd edition rev. 2018.

[13] 'The Care of Women Requesting Induced Abortion', RCOG (November 2011).

[14] theabortionsurvivors.com/abortion-survivors-and-their-stories/sarah-smith/

[15] UK Confidential Inquiry into Maternal Deaths 2008. (After this they stopped keeping a record.)

## Chapter 14

[1] K. Mühlemann, M. Germain, M. Krohn, 'Does abortion increase the risk of intrapartum infection in the following pregnancy? *Epidemiology* 7(2) (March 1996), pp. 194–8. https://www.ncbi.nlm.nih.gov/pubmed/8834561.

# Endnotes

[2] Dr Angela Lanfranchi, Prof. Ian Gentles, Elizabeth Ring-Cassidy, *Complications: Abortion's Impact on Women* (The deVeber Institute for Bioethics and Social Research, 2013), p. 170. Cited in A.J. Boeke, J.E. van Bergen et al., 'The risk of pelvic inflammatory disease associated with uro-genital infection with chlamydia trachomatis; literature review', *Nederlands Tijdschrift voor Geneeskunde* 149(15) (April 2005), pp. 878–84, https://www.ncbi.nlm.nih.gov/ pubmed/15868993.

[3] 'The Care of Women Requesting Induced Abortion', Royal College of Gynaecologists (November 2011) (accessed 15 August 2019). Also in http://patient.co.uk.health/ pelvic-inflammatory-disease-leaflet (accessed 7 August 2017).

[4] Yu D., Wong Y., Cheong Y., Xia E., and Li T., 'Asherman's Syndrome – One Century Later', *Fertility and Sterility* 2008; 89 (4): 759–79. Quoted page 191 in *Complications: Abortion's Impact on Women*, 2nd Edition, 2018.

[5] Ibid.

[6] Prof. Byron Calhoun, MD, OB/GYN, personal to MH November 2018.

[7] Fergusson D., Horwood L. and Boden J., 'Reactions to abortion and subsequent mental health', *British Journal of Psychiatry* 2009; 195 (5): 420–6. Also Ferguson D., Horwood L. and Boden J., 'Evidence from a 30-year longitudinal study', *British Journal of Psychiatry* 2008; 193:444–51.

[8] Fergusson D., Horwood L. and Boden J., 'Does abortion reduce the mental health risks of unwanted or unintended pregnancy? A reappraisal of the evidence', *Australian and New Zealand Journal of Psychiatry* 47(9) (September 2013), pp. 819–27. https://www.ncbi.nlm.nih.gov/pubmed/23553240 (checked 20 April 19). Fergusson was reviewing this finding which had been affirmed in the UK in 2011: 'Induced Abortion and Mental Health: a systematic review of the evidence – full report and consultation table with responses', Academy of Medical Royal Colleges. See also https://cmfblog.org.uk/2019/03/13/ abortiondoes-not-cause-mental-illness-discuss/

[9] Sullins, D.P. Affective and Substance Abuse Disorders Following Abortion by Pregnancy Intention in the United States: A Longitudinal Cohort Study. *Medicina* **2019**, *55*, 741 (accessed 22-11-19).]

[10] Coleman P.K., Reardon D.C., Rue V., and Cougle J., 'History of induced abortion in relation to substance use during subsequent pregnancies carried to term', *American Journal of Obstetrics and Gynecology* 2002;187, pp. 1673–1678 (accessed 18 September 2019).

[11] Case report from one of the authors: a completed suicide by hanging the day after the abortion with a note from the male partner, 'Life without my child is not worth living...'

[12] Gissler M., et al., 'Pregnancy associated deaths in Finland 1987–1994 – definition problems and benefits of record linkage', *Acta Obstetria et Gynaecologica Scandinavica*, 1997; 76 (7), pp. 651–7.

[13] Coleman P., 'Abortion and mental health: quantitative synthesis and analysis of research published 1995–2009', *British Journal of Psychiatry* 2011;199 (3), pp. 180–186 http://doi.org/10.1192/bjp.bp.110.077230

[14] The following paper also reports (table 2) (with 94% confidence) that if the Swedish mother of a preemie child had any IA history, her 'preemie' has 1.6 times the risk of being diagnosed with CP compared to Swedish mothers with no IA history, who are also mothers of preemies, 'Cerebral palsy in preterm infants: a population-based case-control study of antenatal and intrapartal risk factors', B. Jacobsson, G. Hagberg, B. Hagberg, L. Ladfors, A. Niklasson and H. Hagberg, Perinatal Center, Departments of Obstetrics and Gynecology, Sahlgrensk a University Hospital and Departments of Pediatrics, Queen Silvia Children's Hospital, Institute for the Health of Women and Children, Göteborg, Sweden *Acta Paediatrica* 2002; 91: 946–951. Stockholm ISSN 0803-5253

[15] The Care of Women Requesting Induced Abortion', RCOG (November 2011), (accessed 30 April 2019).

[16] W. Zhou, J. Olsen, et al., 'Risk of spontaneous abortion following induced abortion is only increased with short interpregnancy interval', *Journal of Obstetrics and Gynaecology* 20(1) (January 2000): pp. 49–54 https://www.ncbi.nlm.nih.gov/pubmed/15512467. K. Mühlemann, M. Germain, M. Krohn, 'Does abortion increase the risk of intrapartum infection in the following pregnancy?' Epidemiology 7(2) (March 1996), pp. 194–8 https://www.ncbi.nlm.nih.gov/pubmed/8834561

[17] Odds Ratio 4.79 (95% Confidence Interval 1.46–15.68); W. Zhou and J. Olsen, 'Are complications after an induced abortion associated with reproductive failures in a subsequent pregnancy?' *Acta Obstetricia et Gynecologica Scandinavica* 82(2) (February 2003), pp. 177–81 https://www.ncbi.nlm.nih.gov/pubmed/12648182

[18] Odds Ratio 4.79 (95% Confidence Interval 1.46–15.68); W. Zhou and J. Olsen, 'Are complications after an induced abortion associated with reproductive failures in a subsequent pregnancy?' *Acta Obstetricia et Gynecologica Scandinavica* 82(2) (Feb 2003), pp. 177–81 https://www.ncbi.nlm.nih.gov/pubmed/12648182

[19] The Care of Women Requesting Induced Abortion', RCOG (November 2011) (accessed 25 February 2019).

[20] L. Dyan, 'Pelvic inflammatory disease', *Australian Family Physician* 35(11) (2006), p. 861. Quoted in *Complications: Abortion's Impact on Women*, 2013, p. 178.

[21] L. Dyan, 'Pelvic inflammatory disease', *Australian Family Physician* 35(11) (2006), p. 861. Quoted in *Complications: Abortion's Impact on Women*, 2013, p. 178.

[22] Ibid.

[23] Image https://www.shutterstock.com/editor/image/illustration-uterus-ectopic-pregnancy-gynecology-429233158

[24] L.K. Dhaliwal, K.R. Gupta and S. Gopalan, 'Induced abortion and subsequent pregnancy outcome', *Journal of Family Welfare* 49(1) (June 2003), pp. 50–5 https://www. popline.org/node/233271

[25] UK Cancer Registry data supplied by letter, inclusive of Cancer-in-situ, to Patrick arroll PAPRI, 2018.

[26] SEER data (Surveillance, Epidemiology and End Results program of the National Cancer Institute).

[27] D. Trichopoulos, et al., 'Age at any birth and breast cancer risk', *International Journal of Cancer* 31 (15 June 1983), pp. 701–4. Each one-year delay in FFTP increases relative breast cancer risk by 3.5%. These figures kindly interpreted by Dr Robert Dixon, medical statistician Sheffield, 3 March 2017 who added, 'One fifth or 20% is in keeping with the 95% confidence limits of 2.3% to 4.7%' https://onlinelibrary. wiley.com/doi/abs/10.1002/ijc.2910310604 (accessed 15 August 2019).

[28] Achilles S.L. and Reeves M.F., 'Prevention of infection after induced abortion', release date October 2010 SFP guideline 2012. *Contraception* 2012; 83 (4), pp. 295–309. Quoted in page 109–110 *Complications: Abortion's Impact on Women*, 2nd Edition.

[29] Gissler M., Berg C., Bouvier-Colle M.H., Buekens P., 'Methods for identifying pregnancy associated deaths: population-based data from Finland 1987–2000', *Paediatra Perinat Epidemiol* [Internet]. STAKES, Helsinki, Finland; November 2004, Dunlap (checked 8 May 2019).

[30] JAMA, 1999;281(11), pp. 1037–41.

[31] 'Reproductive history patterns and long-term mortality rates: a Danish population-based record linkage study', *European Journal of Public Health* 2012, Volume 23, Number 4, pp. 569-574. Priscilla K. Coleman, Dr David Reardon, Prof. Byron C. Calhoun (citation checked 30 April 2019).

[32] Wokama T.T., et al. (2014) 'A comparative study of the prevalence of domestic violence in women requesting termination of pregnancy and those attending an antenatal clinic', *BJOG* 121:6 to 7-633.

## Chapter 15

[1] Pain of First-trimester Abortion: A Study of Psychosocial and Medical Predictors, E. Bellanger, et al., *Pain* 36:339 (1989). Quoted in Abortion Risks website, differential physical complications of adolescent abortion.

[2] Dr Angela Lanfranchi, Prof. Ian Gentles, Elizabeth Ring-Cassidy, *Complications: Abortion's Impact on Women* ( The deVeber Institute for Bioethics and Social Research,2013).

[3] J. Jeffes, *Unplanned Pregnancy: Talking with Teenagers* (Hove: Lean Press, 2013).

[4] A person known to an author.

[5] G. Condon and D. Hazzard, *Fatherhood Aborted: The Profound Effects of Abortion on Men*, (Carol Stream, IL: T yndale House, 2001). See also http://www.deveber.org/ text/chapters/Chap16.pdf.

[6] Coleman P., 'Resolution of unwanted pregnancy during adolescence through abortion versus childbirth: individual and family predictors and psychological consequences', *Journal of Youth and Adolescence* 2006; 35(6), pp. 903–911.

[7] D. M. Fergusson, L.J. Horwood and E.M. Ridder, 'Abortion in young women and subsequent mental health', JCPP, 2006.

[8] P.K. Coleman, 'Resolution of Unwanted Pregnancy During Adolescence Through Abortion Versus Childbirth: Individual and Family Predictors and Psychological Consequences,' *Journal of Youth and Adolescence* 35(6) (December 2006), pp. 903–911.

[9] N.B. Campbell, K. Franco, S. Jurs, 'Abortion in Adolescence', *Adolescence*, 23(92) (Winter 1998), pp. 813–23. https://www.ncbi.nlm.nih.gov/pubmed/3232570.

[10] B. Garfinkel, et al., 'Stress, depression and suicide: A study of adolescents in Minnesota', University of Minnesota (1986), pp. 43–55.

[11] C. Morgan, M. Evans and J. Peters, 'Suicides after Pregnancy', *BMJ* 314(902) (March 1997), data extracted and plotted from Table 1, pp. 902–3.

[12] Prof XX MD, OBGYN, to the author April 2019.

[13] de Brouwer, Anne-Marie, *Supranational Criminal Prosecution of Sexual Violence: The ICC and the Practice of the ICTY and the ICTR*, (Intersentia, 2005, ISBN:978-90-5095-533-1), https://en.wikipedia.org/wiki/Pregnancy_from_rape#cite_ref-FOOTNOTEde_Brouwer2005225_64-0 (accessed 10 July 2019).

[14] S. Osser and K. Perrson, 'Post Abortal Pelvic Infection Associated with Chlamydia Trachomatis Infection and the Influence of Humoral Immunity', *American Journal of Obstetrics and Gynecology* 150(6) (November 1984), pp. 699–703 http://www.ajog.org/ article/0002-9378(84)90670-7/fulltext.

## Chapter 16

[1] Heard by one of the authors in 2017.

[2] J. Jeffes, *What Happens after an Abortion?* (Hove: Lean Press, 2014).

[3] B. McMahon, 'Play fighting and straight talking: the new science on why dads matter', *The Times* (20 June 2015) http s://www. thetimes.co.uk/article/ play -fighting- and-straight-talking-the-new-science-on-why-dads-matter-ghcswlbhwlp.

[4] A. Kero, A. Lalos, et al., 'The male partner involved in legal abortion', *Human Reproduction* 14(10) (October 1999), pp. 2669–75 http://humrep. oxfordjournals.org/ content/14/10/2669.full (accessed 12 June 2019).

[5] Case report to the author.

[6] Personal to the authors November 2018.

[7] A. Lanfranchi, I. Gentles, E. Ring-Cassidy, *Complications: Abortion's Impact on Women* ( The deVeber Institute for Bioethics and Social Research, 2013).

[8] http://www.menandabortion.com/articles.html (accessed 16 April 2019).

[9] http://www.menandabortion.com/articles.html (accessed 16 April 2019).

[10] L. Bird Franke, *The Ambivalence of Abortion* (New York: Random House, 1978), p. 63. See also, D. Reardon, *Aborted Women, Silent No More* (Good New Publishers, 1987), p. 45.

[11] Dr T. Karminski Burke, 'Can Relationships Survive after Abortion?' http://afterabortion.org/1999/can-relationships-surviveafter-abortion/

[12] Sharon Pearce, 'Can Relationships Survive after an Abortion?' http://www.silentvoices.org/blog/can-relationships-surviveafter-an-abortion (accessed 10 July 2017).

[13] Similar image found at https://www.shutterstock.com/image-photo/portrait-mixed-race-couple-thinking-looking-333778643

[14] Brad Mattes, lecture, Jerusalem, November 2018.

[15] www.menandabortion.net/

## Chapter 17

[1] https://www.bioedge.org/bioethics/are-abortions-for-cleft-palate-rising-in-the-uk/11994

[2] Copyright ©2019 Metro.co.uk

[3] John Wyatt, *Matters of Life and Death* (Nottingham: IVP, 2nd Edition, 2009), p. 84. Dr Fiona Fairlie, fetal medicine specialist wrote, 'I have tried to find accurate data about the chance of an abnormality, but it is difficult... When I was helping women, who had an increased risk of a baby with an abnormality due to the drugs they needed in pregnancy, I gave them a "background" risk of 2–3% for a major abnormality, e.g. spina bifida or major cardiac defect. So, I think 1 in 25, that's 4% is reasonable.' Personal communication 1 June 2017, Sheffield, UK.

[4] Wyatt, *Matters of Life and Death*, 2009.

[5] Prof John Wyatt personal conversation 8-2-20

[6] https://www.nhs.uk/conditions/downs-syndrome/causes/ (accessed 22 July 2019).

[7] http://www.nhs.uk/conditions/Chorionic-Villus-sampling/Pages/Introduction.aspx (accessed 14 June 2017).

[8] 'Non-Invasive Prenatal Testing: Ethical Issues', Nuffield Council on Bioethics (March 2017) http://nuffieldbioethics.org/project/non-invasive-prenatal-testing (accessed 15August 2019).

[9] 'Non-Invasive Prenatal Testing: Ethical Issues'.

[10] National Institute for Clinical Excellence, 'Antenatal Care: Routine Care for the Healthy Pregnant Woman', Clinical Guideline CG62, NICE (March 2008) http://guidance.nice.org.uk/CG62

[11] R. Dodds, 'The stress of tests in pregnancy: an antenatal screening survey', National Childbirth Trust (UK), 1997 (quoted in J. Wyatt, *Matters of Life and Death*, p. 113).

[12] H. Statham, et al., 'Prenatal diagnosis of fetal abnormality: psychological effects on women in low risk pregnancies', *Best Practice & Research Clinical Obstetrics and Gynaecology* 14 (2000), pp. 731–47. (See J. Wyatt, *Matters of Life and Death*, p. 112.)

[13] G. McGee, *The Perfect Baby*, quoted in Wyatt, Matters of Life and Death, 2009, p. 114.

[14] V. Davies, et al., 'Psychological outcome in women undergoing termination of pregnancy for ultrasound-detected fetal anomaly in the first and 2nd trimesters: a pilot study', *Ultrasound in Obstetrics & Gynecology* 25(4) (Apr 2005): pp. 389– 92.

[15] Wyatt, *Matters of Life and Death*, 2009.

[16] C.H. Zeanah, et al., 'Do women grieve after terminating pregnancies because of fetal anomalies? A controlled investigation', *Obstetrics & Gynecology* 82(2) (August 1993), pp. 270–5.

[17] 'A valid and reliable survey of 4,924 households', B.G. Skotko, et al., 'Having a son or daughter with Down's syndrome: perspectives from mothers and fathers', *American Journal of Medical Genetics Part A* 155A(10) (Oct 2011): 2,335–47 (accessed 17 June 2019).

## Part 3

[1] The Care of Women Requesting Induced Abortion', Royal College of Gynaecologists (November 2011).

[2] Dibaba et al., 2013. 'The effects of pregnancy intention on the use of antenatal care services: systematic review and metaanalysis', reproductive health. Shah et al., 2011. 'Intention to become pregnant and low birth weight and preterm birth: a systematic review', *Maternal and Child Health Journal* 15:205–16. Abajobir et al., 2016. 'A systematic review and meta-analysis of the association and unintended pregnancy and perinatal depression'.

# Chapter 18

[1] Fergusson D.M., Horwood L.J., Boden J.M., 'Does abortion reduce the mental health risks of unwanted or unintended pregnancy? A reappraisal of the evidence', *Australian and New Zealand Journal of Psychiatry* 2013; 47, pp. 819–827.

[2] 'Women Who Suffered Emotionally from Abortion: A Qualitative Synthesis of Their Experiences', Priscilla K. Coleman, PhD, Caitlin Boswell, B.S., Katrina Etzkorn, B.S., Rachel Turnwald, B.S.

[3] 'Abortion, substance abuse and mental health in early adulthood. Thirteen-year longitudinal evidence from the United States', Donald Paul Sullins, 23 September 2016, SAGE Open Medicine.

[4] 'Abortion, substance abuse and mental health in early adulthood. Thirteen-year longitudinal evidence from the United States,' Donald Paul Sullins, 23 September 2016, SAGE Open Medicine https://doi.org/10.1177/2050312116665997. This study made their conclusions 'after extensive adjustment for confounding, other pregnancy outcomes, and socio-demographic differences, abortion was consistently associated with increased risk of mental health disorder'.

[5] 'Induced Abortion and Mental Health: A systematic review of the mental health outcomes of induced abortion, including their prevalence and associated factors' evidence-full report and consultation table with responses, Academy of Medical Royal Colleges (December 2011) https://www.aomrc.org.uk/wp-content/uploads/2016/05/Induced_Abortion_Mental_Health_1211.pdf.

[6] D. Fergusson, L.J. Horwood and J. Boden, 'Does abortion reduce the mental health risks of unwanted or unintended pregnancy? A reappraisal of the evidence', *Australian and New Zealand Journal of Psychiatry* 47(9) (September 2013), pp. 1204–1205 https://www.cbi.nlm.nih.gov/pubmed/23553240 (accessed 15 August 2019).

[7] See also W. Pedersen, 'Abortion and depression: a population-based longitudinal study of young women', Scandinavian Journal of Public Health 36(4) (June 2008), pp.424–8 https://www.ncbi.nlm.nih.gov/pubmed/18539697

[8] https://www.rcpsych.ac.uk/mental-health/problems-disorders/post-natal-depression (accessed 15 September 2018).

[9] G. Penny, 'Treatment of pain during medical abortion', *Contraception* 74(1) (July 2006), pp. 45–7.

[10] Also reported to the authors by Prof. Byron Calhoun MD, OB/GYN, West Virginia University, November 2018.

[11] For instance Priscilla K. Coleman, Dr David Reardon and Prof. Byron C. Calhoun, 'Reproductive history patterns and long-term mortality rates: a Danish

population-based record linkage study', *European Journal of Public Health* 2012, Volume 23, Number 4, pp. 569–574 (accessed 30 April 2019).

[12] Brad Mattes, 'Hidden Victims of Abortion', lecture, Jerusalem, Israel, November 2018.

[13] Mattes also quoted among other authorities, Milling, E., 'The Men Who Wait', *Woman's Life* April 1975, pp. 48–49.

[14] A. Lanfranchi, I. Gentles. E. Ring-Cassidy, *Complications: Abortion's Impact on Women*, 2nd Edition, (The deVeber Institute for Bioethics and Social Research, 2018).

## Chapter 19

[1] http://www.who.int/reproductivehealth/topics/infertility/definitions/en/ (accessed 15 June 2019).

[2] http://www.nhs.uk/conditions/Infertility/Pages/Introduction.aspx (accessed 24 May 2017). That's about 1 in 7 couples and in a third of cases it is due to female problems.

[3] https://www.womenshealth.gov/a-z-topics/infertility (accessed 28 August 2019).

[4] M.A. Hassan and S.R. Killick, 'Is previous aberrant reproductive outcome predictive of subsequently reduced fecundity?' *Human Reproduction* 20(3) (March 2005), pp. 657–64. Odds ratio 7.2 (p value 0.02), p. 662. Further evidence in Dr Angela Lanfranchi, Prof. Ian Gentles, Elizabeth Ring-Cassidy, *Complications: Abortion's Impact on Women* ( The deVeber Institute for Bioethics and Social Research, 2013), p. 176.

[5] Y. Che, W. Zhou, E. Gao, J. Olsen, 'Induced abortion and prematurity in a subset pregnancy: a study from Shanghai', *Journal of Obstetrics and Gynaecology* 21(3) (July 2001), pp. 270–3 http://www.tandfonline.com/doi/abs/10.1080/01443610120046396

[6] The relative risk was 2.1, 95% confidence interval 1.1–4.0 after one previous abortion, and relative risk 2.3, 95% confidence interval 1.0–5 point 2:03 previous abortions. A. Tzonou, C.C. Hsieh, D. Trichopoulos, et al., 'Induced abortions, miscarriages, and tobacco smoking as risk factors for secondary infertility', *Journal of Epidemiology and Community Health* 47(1) (February 1993), pp. 36–9.

[7] K. Mühlemann, M. Germain, M. Krohn, 'Does abortion increase the risk of intra-partum infection in the following pregnancy?' *Epidemiology* 7(2) (March 1996), pp. 194–8 https://www.ncbi.nlm.nih.gov/pubmed/8834561 (accessed 17 June 2019).

[8] L. Dyan, 'Pelvic inflammatory disease', *Australian Family Physician* 35(11) (2006), p. 861. Quoted in *Complications: Abortion's Impact on Women*, p. 178.

[9] Ibid.

[10] L. Dyan, 'Pelvic inflammatory disease', *Australian Family Physician* 35(11) (2006), p. 861. Quoted in Complications: Abortion's Impact on Women, p. 178.

[11] *Complications: Abortion's Impact on Women*, 2nd Edition, 2018.

[12] Ibid.

## Chapter 20

[1] Public data kindly plotted by Dr Greg Gardner and Margaret Eames, (FSS,FRSPH, MSc, DLSHTM, PGCE, BSc) Head of Public Health Intelligence, The Acorns Public Health Research Unit, 38, Hazel Grove, Hatfield, Herts AL10 9DN.

[2] K.L. Costeloe, E.M. Hennessy, et al., 'Short-term outcomes after extreme preterm birth in England: comparison of two birth cohorts in 1995 and 2006' (the EPICure studies) *British Medical Journal* https://www.bmj.com/content/345/bmj.e7976 (accessed 18 June 2019)

[3] T. Moore, E.M. Hennessy, et al., 'Neurological and developmental outcome in extremely preterm children born in England in 1995 and 2006 (the EPICure studies) *British Medical Journal* 345(e7961) (December 2012) (accessed 16 August 2019) https://www.bmj.com/content/345/bmj.e7961

[4] P.S. Shah, J. Zao, 'Induced termination of pregnancy and low birth weight and preterm birth: a systematic review and metaanalyses, *British Journal of Obstetrics & Gynaecology* 116 (October 2009), pp. 1425–42 https://www.ncbi. nlm.nih.gov/pubmed/19769749 (accessed 28 August 2019).

[5] G. Saccone, L. Perriera, V. Berghella, 'Prior uterine evacuation of pregnancy as independent risk factor for preterm birth: a systematic review and meta-analysis', *American Journal Obstetrics & Gynecology* 214(5) (May 2016), pp. 572–91 www.ajog.org/article/S0002-9378(15)02596-X/abstract (accessed 18 June 2019).

[6] E. Lieberman, K.J. Ryan, R.R. Monson, S.C. Schoenbaum, 'Risk factors accounting for racial differences in the rate of premature birth', *New England Journal of Medicine* 317(12) (September 1987), pp. 743–8 http://www.nejm.org/doi/ pdf/10.1056/ (accessed 16 August 2019).

[7] H.M. Swingle, T.T. Colaizy, M.B. Zimmerman, F.H. Morriss, 'Abortion and the risk of subsequent preterm birth', *Journal of Reproductive Medicine* 54(2) (February 2009), pp. 95–108 https://www.ncbi.nlm.nih.gov/pubmed/19301572

[8] C. Moreau, M. Kaminski, P.Y. Ancel, et al., 'Previous induced abortion and the risk of very preterm delivery: results of the EPIPAGE study', *British Journal of Obstetrics & Gynaecology* 112(4) (April 2005), pp. 430–7 https://www.ncbi.nlm. nih.gov/pu- bmed/15777440

[9] Communication from two British authors publishing 2020

[10] Dr Greg Gardner, comments on NHS Choices claims in March 2019: 'NHS Choices made much of the Klemetti paper not showing a statistically significant increase in *moderate* preterm birth after one or two abortions, only *after three.* One of the issues with *all the* papers from Finland is that the comparison group used is primiparous women (first time births). We know from the companion Raisanen study in 2013, with a massive 1.4 million women, that the risk of PTB in primiparous women (in Finland at least) is huge. If you compare women who aborted their first pregnancy with women giving birth for the first time (who already have a high risk of PTB) you won't show much of an increased risk. The correct comparison group should be women whose first pregnancy went to term. Table 2 in Raisanen shows the increased risk of PTB in primiparous women for moderate PTB (over 32 weeks) is already at 1.49 (1.46–1.52). No wonder they can't show much of an increased risk at this gestation.'

[11] K. Mühlemann, M. Germain, M. Krohn, 'Does abortion increase the risk of intrapartum infection in the following pregnancy? *Epidemiology* 7(2) (March 1996), pp. 194–8 https://www.ncbi.nlm.nih.gov/pubmed/8834561

[12] P.Y. Ancel, et al., 'History of induced abortion as a risk factor for preterm birth in European countries: results of the EUROPOP survey', *Human Reproduction* 19(3) (March 2004), pp. 734–40 https://www.ncbi.nlm.nih.gov/pubmed/14998979 (accessed 28 August 2019).

[13] Ancel, et al., 'History of induced abortion as a risk factor for preterm birth in European countries' *Human Reproduction*, 2004.

[14] Mangham L.J., et al., 'The cost of preterm birth throughout childhood in England and Wales', *Pediatrics* 2009

Feb;123(2): e312–27 estimated costs to the NHS of neo-natal care for preterm birth at £2.946 billion in 2006. Allowing for inflation, this amount is likely over £3.8 billion in 2018. (Figures kindly supplied by Margaret Eames FSS, FRSPH, MSc, DLSHTM he, PGCE, BSc, Head of Public Health Intelligence, The Acorns Public Health Research Unit, Herts AL10 9DN, email to the author 31 January 2018.)

M. Eames with an economist, email 10 November 2017, 'Recent papers show that a higher relative risk of 1.62 extremely preterm infants among those who have had surgical abortion compared to those who have not, means an attributable risk of about 245 additional infants per year born in the UK at less than 28 weeks due to abortion.' *This calculated as follows:*

Using 1) the 2016 actual figures (for total births in the UK, and Scottish data (which is more accurate than English) for rate of very preterm births (vPTB) and extremely preterm birth (xPTB).

Using 2) the estimate of 1085 PTBs in UK = 1% (rate of vPTB births) x 14% (woman in delivery who have had abortion) x 774000 (all births in UK in 2016) and a relative risk of 1.3 for increased risk of vPTB for mothers who had abortions compared with those who have had none, we find that:

a) In the UK – 325 extra babies (30% x 1085) are likely to be being born under 32 weeks (very Preterm births) due to prior abortion. Also using this cautious estimate of relative risk (Adjusted RR=1.3) for extremely PTB would give 118 extra extremely PTBs (x PTB) due to abortion i.e. 217/597- (the Scottish ratio of xPTB/all vPTB) x 0.3 x1085).

b) However, using the more recent relative risk of 1.62 (as published in Bhattacharya, 2013, or 1.56 in Raisanen, 2013) for x PTB would give **245 extra** extremely preterm births due to abortion. See Bhattacharya S., Lowit A., Raja E.A., Lee A.J., Mahmood T., Templeton A., 'Reproductive outcomes following induced abortion: a national register-based cohort study in Scotland', *BMJ Open*, 2012;2(4). And see Raisanen S., Gissler M., Saari J., Kramer M., Heinonen S., 'Contribution of risk factors to extremely, very and moderately preterm births – register-based analysis of 1,390,742 singleton births', PLoS One, 2013;8(4):e60660.

[15] B.C. Calhoun, E. Shadigian, B. Rooney, 'Cost consequences of induced abortion as an attributable risk for preterm birth and impact on informed consent', *Journal of Reproductive Medicine* 52(10) (October 2007), pp. 929–37 https://www.ncbi.nlm.nih. gov/pubmed/17977168 (accessed 10 July 2019).

# Chapter 21

[1] Dr Mary L. Davenport, MD, FACOG, Adjunct Clinical Assistant Professor of Obstetrics and Gynecology, College of Osteopathic Medicine, Touro University, Vice President, Breast Cancer Prevention Institute; Angela Lanfranchi, MD, FACS, Clinical Assistant Professor of Surgery, Rutgers-Robert Wood, Johnson Medical School, President, Breast Cancer Prevention Institute. Lecture, Indianapolis, April 2019.

[2] Cancer Research UK, https://www.cancerresearchuk.org/health-professional/our-reports-and-publications (accessed 18 June 2019).

[3] https://www.breasthealthuk.com/about-breast-cancer/breast-cancer-survival-rates (accessed 14 February 2017).

[4] P.S. Carroll, J.S. Utshudiema, J. Rodrigues, 'The British breast cancer epidemic: trends, patterns, risk factors, and forecasting', *Journal of American Physicians and Surgeons* 22(1) (Spring 2017). One in 7 confirmed in a letter to Patrick Carroll from Cancer Research UK, 8 August 2017 who recalculated latest statistics to 1 in 7.14 women, which is like Carroll's published paper. (Cancer Research UK round their figures up but they are reviewing this.) Adding in the in-situ cancers as well gives a figure of 1 woman in 6 for lifetime risk.

[5] Lei Fan et al. Breast cancer in a transitional society over 18 years: trends and present status in Shanghai, China. Breast Cancer Research and Treatment 2009;117;409-416 (accessed 28-11-19)

[6] 1. Nilsen B.C., Waldenstron U., et al., 'Characteristics of women who are pregnant with their first baby at an advanced age', *Acta Obstetrica Gynecologica Scandinavica* 2012; 91: 353–362.

2. Henriet L., Kaminski M., 'Impact of induced abortions on subsequent pregnancy outcome: the 1995 French national perinatal survey', *British Journal of Obstetrics and Gynaecology* 2001;108(10), pp. 1036–1042.

[7] Breast cancer risk increase due to raised age at first full-term pregnancy, three references: (A) E. Negri, et al., 'Risk factors for breast cancer: pooled results from three Italian case-control studies', *American Journal of Epidemiology* 128(6) (December 1988), pp. 1207–15 https://www.ncbi.nlm.nih.gov/pubmed/3195562. The 'Negri' study can be considered a small meta-analysis; first full-term pregnancy after age 28 imparts 1.8 times the B.C. risk versus first full-term pregnancy under age 22.

(B) J. Wohlfahrt, M. Melbye, 'Age at any birth is associated with breast cancer risk', *Epidemiology* 12(1) (January 2001,) pp. 68–73

https://journals.lww.com/epidem/Fulltext/2001/01000/Age_at_Any_Birth_Is_Associated_with_Breast_Cancer.12.aspx (accessed 16 August 2019).

(C) D. Trichopoulos, et al., 'Age at any birth and breast cancer risk', *International Journal of Cancer* 31 (15 June 1983), pp 701–4

https://onlinelibrary.wiley.com/doi/abs/10.1002/ijc.2910310604 (accessed 16 August 2019). Each one-year delay in FFTP increases relative breast cancer risk by 3.5%.

[8] This guide figure for the 18-year-old woman is based on a personal communication to the author from Brent Rooney in 2017 who calculated it from the following paper where each ane-year delay in first full-term pregnancy increases relative breast cancer risk by 3.5%. D. Trichopoulos, et al., 'Age at any birth and breast cancer risk', *International Journal of Cancer* 31 (15 June 1983), pp. 701–4 http://onlinelibrary.wiley.com/ doi/10.1002/ijc.2910310604/abstract (accessed 14 June 2017).

[9] D. Trichopoulos, et al., 'Age at any birth and breast cancer risk', *International Journal of Cancer* 31 (15 June 1983), pp. 701–4. http://onlinelibrary.wiley.com/doi/10.1002/ijc.2910310604/abstract (accessed 14 June 2017). Each one-year delay in FFTP increases relative breast cancer risk by 3.5%.

[10] B. Nilsen, U. Waldenstron, et al., 'Characteristics of women who are pregnant with their first baby at an advanced age', *Acta Obstetricia Gynecologica Scandinavica* 91(3) (March 2012), pp. 353–62. Comment by Brent Rooney to the author in 2017:

# Endnotes

'This large 2012 Anne Nilsen et al. study of women in Norway looked for factors associated with "women who are pregnant with their first baby at an advanced age." The researchers subdivided their study subjects into three maternal age categories (25–32 years, 33–37, over age 37). If a Norwegian woman had induced abortion history, she was 70% more likely to be have a maternal age *at first birth* between 33 and 37 than women with no prior IAs and 90% more likely to have maternal age over 37 years than women with no prior IAs.'

[11] www.publications.parliament.uk/pa/cm200607/cmselect/cmsctech/1045/1045we15.htm.

[12] Melbye M., Wohlfahrt J., Anderson A.M.N., Westergaard T. and Andersen P.K., 'Premature delivery and breast cancer risk', *British Journal of Cancer* 1999 April; 80:609–13. Also see Vatten L.J., Trichopoulos D., et al., 'Pregnancy-related protection against breast cancer depends on length of gestation', *British Journal of Cancer* 2002 July; 87:289-90.

[13] Department of Gynaecology and Obstetrics University of Zürich, Switzerland.

[14] Data and interpretation kindly supplied April 2019 by Angela Lanfranchi MD FACS, President, Breast Cancer Prevention Institute, and Mary Davenport MD FACOG, Vice President, Breast Cancer Prevention Institute.

[15] Brind J., Condly S.J., Lanfranchi A., Rooney B., 'Induced abortion as an independent risk factor for breast cancer: a systematic review and meta-analysis of studies of South Asian women', *Issues in Law and Medicine,* Spring 2018.

[16] Huang Y., Zhang X., Li W. et al., 'Cancer Causes Control' (2014) 25: 227. https://doi.org/10.1007/s10552-013-0325-7 (accessed 6 May 2019).

[17] J. Epidemiol, 2019; 29 (5): 173–179, 'Induced abortion, birth control methods, and breast cancer risk: case-control study in China'. Analysis is needed and numbers are too small to be conclusive as yet.

[18] V. Beral, et al., 'Collaborative Group on Hormonal Factors in Breast Cancer. Breast cancer and abortion: collaborative reanalysis of data from 53 epidemiological studies, including 83,000 women with breast cancer from 16 countries', *The Lancet* 363(9414) (2004), pp. 1007–16.

[19] All listed at www.choicescommunity.com

[20] List of ABC Link studies found at Breast Cancer Research Institute www.bcpinstitute.org under Resources Tab, under Fact Sheets (accessed May 2019).

[21] Figure 17-10 odds ratios for the risk of breast cancer in unit parous women of various ages at delivery, according to the number of years since delivery (Lambe M., Hsieh C.C., Trichopolous D., et al., 'Transient increase in the risk of breast cancer after giving birth', New England Journal of Medicine 331:5-9, 1994. Interpreted and supplied by Dr Angela Lanfranchi MD and Mary Davenport MD, April 2019.

[22] Huang Y., Zhang X., Li W. et al., 'Cancer Causes Control' (2014) 25: 227 https://doi.org/10.1007/s10552-013-0325-7 (accessed 6 May 2019).

[23] A.R. Jiang, C.M. Gao, J.H. Ding, et al., 'Abortions and breast cancer risk in premenopausal and postmenopausal women in Jiangsu Province of China', *Asian Pacific Journal of Cancer Prevention* 13(1) (2012), pp. 33–5. Quoted in p. 115 and later in book from deVeber 2013, Complications: Abortion's Impact on Women.

[24] Ibid.

[25] Lecture by surgical breast specialist Dr Iman Azmy MBBS, Chesterfield, England on 26 January 2016, figures based on the Million Women Study.

[26] V. Beral, et al., 'Collaborative Group on Hormonal Factors in Breast Cancer. Breast cancer and abortion: collaborative reanalysis of data from 53 epidemiological studies, including 83,000 women with breast cancer from 16 countries', *The Lancet* 363(9414) (2004), pp. 1007–16.

[27] publications.parliament.uk/pa/cm200607/cmselect/cmsctech/cmsctech.htm (accessed 6 August 2019).

[28] Möller, et al., 2008, 'Breast cancer and breastfeeding: collaborative reanalysis of individual data from 47 epidemiological studies in 30 countries, including 50,302 women with breast cancer and 96,973 women without the disease', *The Lancet* 360(9328) (2002), p. 187–95 https://lup.lub.lu.se/search/publication/1123899

[29] D. Wahlberg, 'Study: breast cancer not tied to abortion', *Atlanta Journal Constitution*, 26 March 2004. Quoted in A. Lanfranchi, I. Gentles, E. Ring-Cassidy, *Complications: Abortion's Impact on Women.*

[30] See for instance http://www.aaplog.org/wp-content/uploads/2010/02/Induced-Abortion-and-Subsequent-Breast-Cancer-Risk1.pdf (accessed 6 May 2019).

[31] https://annals.org/aim/article-abstract/2718682/breast-cancer-risk-after-recent-childbirth-pooled-analysis-15-prospective (accessed 25 February 2019), 1 January 2019, 'Breast cancer risk after recent childbirth: a pooled analysis of 15 prospective studies', Hazel B. Nichols, PhD et al., *Annals of Internal Medicine.*

[32] Email to author, 30-3-19, 'That's why the Tang study (Tang M.-T. C., Weiss N.S., Malone K., 'Induced abortion in relation to breast cancer among parous women: a birth certificate registry study', *Epidemiology* 2000; 11:177-180) found no risk increase because women with abortion were compared with women with childbirth at the average age of 33, with the mean age at diagnosis of 38: Right at the peak of the transient risk increase with late age at FFTP (OR = 1.3-1.4, just like the OR for abortion). The answer follows quite simply from considering the limitations of the prospective study population and an obvious source of confounding. Specifically, it has been well established that there is a transient increase in breast cancer risk in women giving birth at ages beyond their mid-

twenties, with the maximal increase observed within 5 years post-partum, and the effect disappearing entirely within 15 years post-partum. The magnitude of this transient effect of full-term pregnancy (FTP) is in the same range as that generally reported for induced abortion (RR = 1.2-1.5), but its timing is quite different. That is, it is generally thought that the surge of growth-promoting oestrogen during a full-term pregnancy stimulates the growth of small malignant or premalignant tumours already present in the breast.

Stated another way, women with recent childbirth and a history of induced abortion were being compared to a group – women with recent childbirth and no history of abortion – whose members were at similarly elevated risk. Therefore, the Tang study cohort was simply unsuitable for the measurement of the effect of induced abortion on breast cancer risk.' *Joel Brind, PhD,* President and CEO, Natural Food Science, LLC. See also 2005 review http://www.jpands. org/vol10no4/brind.pdf

[33] Odds ratios for the risk of breast cancer in uniparous women of various ages at delivery; according to the number of years since delivery. Lambe M., Hsieh C.C., Trichopolous D. et al., 'Transient increase in the risk of breast cancer after giving birth', *New England Journal of Medicine* 331:5-9, 1994.

[34] Thanks to Mary L. Davenport, MD and Angela Lanfranchi, MD, lecture in Indianapolis, April 2019.

[35] The biology is well explained in *Complications: Abortion's Impact on Women,* 2nd Edition. Papers on tissue changes, Russo J., Rivera R., Russo I.H., 'Influence of Age and Parity on Development of the Human Breast', *Breast Cancer Research and Treatment* 1992; 23:211–8. Russo J., et al., chapter 1: 'Developmental, Cellular, and Molecular Basis of Human Breast Cancer', *Journal of the National Cancer Institute* monograph 2000; 27:17–37.

[36] Table adapted thanks to Mary L. Davenport, MD and Angela Lanfranchi, MD, lecture in Indianapolis, April 2019.

[37] Data and interpretation kindly supplied April 2019 by Angela Lanfranchi, MD FACS, President, Breast Cancer Prevention Institute, and Mary Davenport, MD FACOG, Vice President, Breast Cancer Prevention Institute.

[38] Image: Mary L. Davenport, MD, FACOG, Adjunct Clinical Assistant Professor of Obstetrics and Gynecology College of Osteopathic Medicine, Touro University, Vice President, Breast Cancer Prevention Institute; Angela Lanfranchi, MD, FACS, Clinical Assistant Professor of Surgery Rutgers-Robert Wood Johnson Medical School, President, Breast Cancer Prevention Institute.

[39] Adapted from data kindly supplied April 2019 by Angela Lanfranchi, MD FACS, President, Breast Cancer Prevention Institute, and Mary Davenport, MD FACOG, Vice President, Breast Cancer Prevention Institute.

[40] C.C. Hsieh, J. Wuu, et al., 'Delivery of premature newborns and maternal breast-cancer risk', *The Lancet* 353(9160) (April 1999), p. 1239. Quoted and well explained in A. Lanfranchi, I. Gentles, E. Ring-Cassidy, *Complications: Abortion's Impact on Women.*

[41] Data and interpretation kindly supplied April 2019 by Angela Lanfranchi, MD FACS, President, Breast Cancer Prevention Institute, and Mary Davenport, MD FACOG, Vice President, Breast Cancer Prevention Institute.

[42] http://www.nhs.uk/Conditions/Cancer-of-the-breast-female/Pages/Causes.aspx.

[43] P.S. Carroll, J.S. Utshudiema, J. Rodrigues, 'The British breast cancer epidemic: trends, patterns, risk factors, and forecasting', *Journal of American Physicians and Surgeons* 22(1) (Spring 2017).

[44] National Cancer Registry Ireland, 2016, http://www.ncri.ie/publications/cancer-trends-and-projections/cancer-trends-29-breast-cancer (accessed 10 August 2017).

[45] Office of National Statistics, 2014, incidence of and mortality from malignant neoplasm of the breast 2004–2014 (accessed 10 August 2017).

[46] Carroll P.S., Utshudiema J.S., Rodrigues J., 'The British breast cancer epidemic: trends, patterns, risk factors, and forecasting' *Journal of American Physicians and Surgeons,* 2017;22(1):8–16. Carroll's paper is mentioned in the growing breast cancer in Pakistan in the peer-reviewed https://bmcpublichealth.biomedcentral.com/articles/10.1186/s12889-019-7330-z

[47] P. Carroll, *Ireland's Gain: The Demographic Impact and Consequences for the Health of Women of the Abortion Laws in Ireland and Northern Ireland* (London: Pension and Population Research Institute, 2011).

[48] Personal discussion with Patrick Carroll, 8 April 2019.

[49] Carroll published 2017, confirming the rising numbers and abortion as part of the problem. P.S. Carroll, J.S. Utshudiema, J. Rodrigues, 'The British breast cancer epidemic: trends, patterns, risk factors, and forecasting', *Journal of American Physicians and Surgeons* 22(1) (Spring 2017).

[50] M. Lambe, C.C. Hsieh, H. Chan, A. Ekbom, D. Trichopolous and H. Adami, 'Parity, age at first and last birth, and risk of breast cancer: a population-based study in Sweden', *Breast Cancer Research and Treatment* 38(3) (January 1996), pp. 305–11 https://www.ncbi.nlm.nih.gov/pubmed/8739084

[51] Data and interpretation kindly supplied April 2019 by Angela Lanfranchi, MD FACS, President, Breast Cancer Prevention Institute and Mary Davenport, MD FACOG, Vice President, Breast Cancer Prevention Institute.

[52] *Complications: Abortion's Impact on Women,* pp. 123–128. Sir Austin Bradford Hill established these criteria in 1964 and used them to show that lung cancer was caused by cigarettes.

Endnotes

[53] https://breast-cancer-research.biomedcentral.com/articles/10.1186/s13058-016-0799-9 (accessed 16 June 2019).

## Chapter 22

[1] Questions to Parliament 20 October 2017 http://www.parliament.uk/business/publications/written-questions-answersstatements/written-question/Commons/2017-10-13/107648/ http://www.parliament.uk/business/publications/writtenquestions-answers-statements/written-question/Commons/2017-10-13/107679/

[2] D.C. Reardon, P.K. Coleman, 'Short- and long-term mortality rates associated with first pregnancy outcome: population register-based study for Denmark 1980–2004', *Medical Science Monitor*18(9) (September 2012), pp. 71–6 http s:// www.ncbi.nlm.nih.go v/ pubmed/22936199 (accessed April 2019).

[3] D.C. Reardon, P.K. Coleman, 'Short- and long-term mortality rates associated with first pregnancy outcome: population register-based study for Denmark 1980–2004', *Medical Science Monitor* 18(9) (September 2012): pp. 71–6. http s://www.ncbi.nlm.nih.go v/ pubmed/22936199

[4] D.C. Reardon, P.G. Ney, et al., 'Deaths associated with pregnancy outcome: A record linkage study of low-income women', *Southern Medical Journal* 95(8) (August 2002), pp. 834–41 http s://www.ncbi.nlm.nih.go v/pubmed/12190217 (accessed April 2019).

[5] Ibid.

[6] Kaunitz A.M., 'Causes of maternal mortality in the United States', *Obstetrics and Gynecology* 1985; 65, pp. 605-612, quoted by Prof. Byron Calhounm, MD, FACOG, Professor and Vice Chair, Department of Obstetrics and Gynaecology, West Virginia University Charleston, WV in *Issues in Law and Medicine*, volume 30, number 2, 2015.

[7] Gissler M., Berg C., Bouvier-Colle M.H., Buekens P., 'Methods for identifying pregnancy associated deaths: population-based data from Finland 1987–2000, Paediatra Perinat Epidemiol (Internet). STAKES, Helsinki, Finland; November 2004. Dunlap (accessed 8 May 8 2019).

[8] Data points by Reardon D, from: Gissler M, et al, Methods for identifying pregnancy associated deaths: Population-based data from Finland 1987-2000. Paediatr Perinat Epidemiol. 2004;18(6):448-455; Table 5.

[9] M. Gissler, C. Berg, et al., 'Injury deaths, suicides and homicides associated with pregnancy, Finland 1987–2000', *European Journal of Public Health* 15(5) (October 2005), pp. 459–63 https://www.ncbi.nlm.nih.gov/pubmed/16051655

[10] M. Gissler, E. Hemminki, J. Lonnqvist, 'Suicides after pregnancy in Finland, 1987–94: register linkage study', *British Medical Journal* 313 (December 1996),

pp. 1431–34 http://www.bmj.com/content/313/7070/1431

[11] Gissler M., Berg C., Bouvier-Colle M.H., Buekens P., 'Injury deaths, suicides and homicides associated with pregnancy, Finland, 1987–2000', *EJPH* 15(5) (October 2005) (accessed 8 May 2019).

[12] M. Gissler, E. Hemminki, J. Lonnqvist, 'Suicides after pregnancy in Finland, 1987–94: register linkage study', *British Medical Journal* 313 (December 1996), pp. 1431–34 http://www.bmj.com/content/313/7070/1431 (accessed 8 May 2019).

[13] D.C. Reardon, P.G. Ney, et al., 'Deaths associated with pregnancy outcome: A record linkage study of low-income women', *Southern Medical Journal* 95(8) (August 2002), pp. 834–41 https://www.ncbi.nlm.nih.gov/pubmed/12190217 (accessed 8 May 2019).

[14] D.C. Reardon, P.G. Ney, et al., 'Deaths associated with pregnancy outcome: A record linkage study of low-income women', *Southern Medical Journal* 95(8) (August 2002), pp. 834–41 https://www.ncbi.nlm.nih.gov/pubmed/12190217 (accessed 8 May 2019).

[15] M. Gissler, C. Berg, et al., 'Pregnancy-associated mortality after birth, spontaneous abortion, or induced abortion in Finland, 1987–2000', *American Journal of Obstetrics & Gynecology* 190(2) (February 2004), pp. 422–7 (accessed 8 May 2019).

[16] https://journals.plos.org/plosone/article?id=10.1371/journal.pone.0036613. Discussion with the author 7 August 2019 and accessed 9 April 2019. This study was criticised, so Koch did another one comparing abortion in different Mexican states with different laws, see next.

[17] Accessed 9 April 2019 after discussion with the author. When Blair J. Darney et al. criticised this paper in *Contraception* journal, they were forced to retract a year later when they were shown to have been biased and used 6 methodological flaws: https://www.contraceptionjournal.org/article/S0010-7824(16)30379-1/abstract (accessed 9 April 2019).

[18] Reardon D.C., Thorp J.M., SAGE Open Med. 2017 Nov 13;5:2050312117740490. doi: 10.1177/2050312117740490. eCollection 2017. http://www.abortionrisks.org/index.php?title=Abortion_and_Maternal_Mortality (accessed 29 August 2019)

# Appendix 1

[1] Prof. Lauris Kalduan, MD, PhD, lecture Indianapolis, 4 April 2019.

[2] Jonathan Haidt examines these instinctive moral foundations in all cultures in his 2013 book *The Righteous Mind: Why Good People are Divided by Politics and Religion* (Pantheon, 2012).

[3] H.G. Koenig, D.E. King, V. Benner Carson, *Handbook of Religion and Health* (New York: Oxford University Press, 2nd edition).

[4] http://www.prolifehumanists.org/

[5] https://www.reddit.com/r/DebateAnAtheist/comments/2tuqix/when_does_human_life_begin/ (accessed 16 August 2019).

[6] https://www.reddit.com/r/DebateAnAtheist/comments/2tuqix/when_does_human_life_begin/ (accessed 16 August 2019).

[7] https://www.reddit.com/r/DebateAnAtheist/comments/2tuqix/when_does_human_life_begin/ (accessed 10 August 2017). http://www.businessdictionary.com/definition/utilitarianism.html (accessed 14 June 2017).

[8] Taken from D. Gill, *World Religions: The essential reference guide to the world's major faiths,* (London: HarperCollins, 2003).

[9] A. Lanfranchi, I. Gentles, E. Ring-Cassidy, *Complications: Abortion's Impact on Women* (The deVeber Institute for Bioethics and Social Research, 2013).

[10] http://www.bbc.co.uk/religion/religions/buddhism/buddhistethics/abortion.shtml (accessed 17 May 2017).

[11] http://www.bbc.co.uk/religion/religions/buddhism/buddhistethics/abortion.shtml (accessed 17 May 2017).

[12] Scripture quotes are taken from the Holy Bible, New International Version (Anglicised edition) copyright ©1979, 1984, 2011 by Biblica. Used by permission of Hodder & Stoughton, an Hachette UK company. All rights reserved.

[13] Genesis 1:26–27.

[14] The full story is in Luke 15:11–32.

[15] The earliest church fathers made abortion forbidden. It was Augustine in later times who lapsed into speculation about when the soul was in the unborn human. While the biblical position on the sanctity of life from conception is clear, some Christians have been misled by poor translations of a few verses in Exodus 21:22–25. These made some think God attached less value to a miscarriage, caused by a fight, than to a full-term baby born dead due to the fight. The correct translation of the original Hebrew is captured by the New International Version (NIV Study Bible, 2011) saying, 'If people are fighting and hit the pregnant woman and she gives birth prematurely but there is no

serious injury, the offender must be fined whatever the woman's husband demands and the court allows. But if there is serious injury, you are to take *life for life*... ' So, a baby born dead as a miscarriage meant the death penalty for the opponent in the fight – life for life, just as if the child was born dead as a stillbirth.

[16] John 8:1–11.

[17] http://www.bbc.co.uk/religion/religions/hinduism/hinduethics/abortion_1.shtml (accessed 16 August 2019).

[18] Dr Katrina Riddell, *Islam and the Secularisation of Population Policies: Muslim States and Sustainability* (London: Ashgate, 2009).

[19] Shaleena's full story can be found in Angela Lanfranchi, Ian Gentles, Elizabeth Ring-Cassidy, *Complications: Abortion's Impact on Women*, p. 320.

[20] http://www.bbc.co.uk/schools/gcsebitesize/rs/death/sikhbeliefrev2.shtml (accessed 10 August 2017).

[21] http://www.nhs-chaplaincy-spiritualcare.org.uk/MultiFaith/multifaithresourceforhealthcarechaplains.pdf (accessed 11 November 2015).

[22] Personal conversation 9 April 2019.

[23] Genesis 1:27.

[24] Genesis 4:11.

[25] Rabbi Jonathan Sacks, 'The courage not to conform' http://rabbisacks.org/lech-lecha-5774-the-courage-not-to-conform/ (7 October 2013, accessed 19 August 2019).

[26] Jeremiah 1:5.

[27] Isaiah 49:1.

[28] Psalm 51:14, 17.

[29] Matthew 22:43–45.

[30] See John 3:16–17.

[31] John 6:37.

[32] Luke 23:4.

## Appendix 2

[1] Lie, Robson and May, 2008, 'Experiences of abortion: a narrative review of qualitative studies', BMC Health Services Research.

[2] Williams et al., 2001, 'Pregnancy wantedness: attitude stability over time', *Social Biology* 48:212–33, quoted in 'Continuation of Unintended Pregnancy', Ayerbe et al., Department of Public Health and Primary Care, University of

Cambridge, *The Linacre Quarterly*, sagepub.com/journals-permissions DOI: 10, 1177/0024363919838368

[3] 'We are not affiliated with any Jewish denomination, political organisation, or the messianic movement and we are a 501(c)(3) educational organisation. We inspire Jews to welcome pre-born Jewish children into the inclusive movement of modern Jewish life and religion. We also provide adoption referrals. We teach our community and provide support to Jewish women and men who suffer from post-abortion syndrome. Exodus 34:6–7: *"Adonai, Adonai, compassionate and gracious, slow to anger, abundant in kindness and truth... who preserves kindness for a thousand generations, who forgives iniquity, sin and error, and who cleanses."'*

## Glossary

[1] https://www.cqc.org.uk/news/stories/cqc-inspects-termination-pregnancy-services.

[2] For example https://www.cqc.org.uk/location/1-130902809/inspection-summary#safe.

[3] https://www.biology-online.org/dictionary/Pregnancy (accessed 22 February 2019).

## Further Resources and Reading

[1] www.afterabortion.org

[2] www.aaplog.org phone: 616-546-2639

[3] https://www.bcpinstitute.org/about.html